Making Contracts Work

WOODSLANE

Woodslane Press
Unit 7/5 Vuko Place
Warriewood NSW 2102 Australia
Email: info@woodslane.com.au
Website: www.woodslane.com.au

Making Contracts Work
Published by Woodslane Press in 2010

National Library of Australia Cataloguing-in-Publication entry

Author: Honig, Beverley.

Title: Making contracts work : combining the science of effective procurement with the art of managing supplier relations / Beverley Honig.

Edition: 1st ed.
ISBN: 9781921606885 (pbk.)
Notes: Includes index.
Subjects: Contracts.
            Commercial law.

Dewey Number: 346.02

Design and layout by Vanessa Wilton, Billy Boy Design

Printed in China through Colorcraft Ltd, Hong Kong.

Making Contracts Work

Combining the science of effective procurement with the art of managing supplier contracts

By Beverley Honig BA,LLB,MBA

WOODSLANE

Dedication

This book is dedicated to my loving husband, Jerrold Lichtig, for supporting and encouraging me, being my rock, and for giving me the time to express myself, and to my darling sons, Matthew and Edward, for being there and for keeping me focused on what really matters.

Contents

Foreword

What I most like about this book is its 'practicality' and its way of presenting quite complex ideas in a straightforward, clear and simple manner. Ms Honig's Contract Management Methodology provides a comprehensive system which managers can follow and implement to good effect. Ms Honig is right to point out the importance of effective contract management. Over the past 100 years, business has moved from significant vertical integration towards much more specialisation, with outsourcing occurring in ever increasing places and ways. Hence the art and science of getting what you want done through arranging for other firms to do part of it is more important than ever. The emphasis in this book on planning and on aligning the contract with strategic priorities is most useful. Once these strategic elements are well settled, then the nuts and bolts of contracts are much more likely to deliver a good result. This key topic is well treated in the book.

There are some terrific pearls of wisdom in this book, such as "Remember, suppliers become part of the corporate 'extended family'." This is a most useful idea, which many of us tend to forget! How many of us saw outsourcing contracts, for information systems and processing for example, go very badly, because the outsourcing contract was seen as a panacea for our IS and IT problems, which turned out not to be the case at all? The book is also full of useful tips: from planning, to contract management to effective negotiation. I am confident that even the most experienced contract managers will learn some useful things through reading this book, and that it will increase their effectiveness.

I commend this book to potential readers because it is both rich in its concepts and very practical, with understandable case studies that seem clearly based on stark reality. The thoughtfulness of the approach is compelling, and through applying the principles and practices herein, managers should be able to improve a major part of their business effectiveness; that part related to contracts. It might also well be, that through more effectively contracting, the propensity to contract further, through contracting better, will occur, resulting in even more business benefits!

Finally, the summaries and the checklist in Chapter 10 should be front and centre on every contract manager's desk, as an aid to ensuring comprehensiveness and strategic alignment and focus of their contracts.

Professor Danny Samson
Chair in Management
The University of Melbourne

Preface

Until now, there has been no book on the market that sets out structures and strategies for sound commercial contract management. This book aims to do more than this: it aligns the science of sourcing and procuring of suppliers with the art of smart contract management and works out ways to blend the cultural divide. It does so based on the author's commercial prowess, sound knowledge of global markets and keen understanding of commercial deal making, flanked by the legal pillars that maintain governance in an otherwise chaotic state of variation.

The book is written in a structured way that allows business managers to manage contracts in a holistic manner, understanding and planning the reasons for seeking a contract before the suppliers are selected and before negotiations take shape.

Contract management is seen, for the first time, as a four-stage process (from 'plan' to 'procure' to 'management' to 'review') so that all the layers can be peeled away to shape the best fit supply chain. This book shapes next practice on a global scale in a very real and pragmatic way, using examples and case studies for illustration. By doing so, it sets out to be at once a guide, a business coach and a form of handbook for any manager - or indeed supplier - working in any part of this supply chain.

Introduction

Everyone at some stage of their working life has been or will be involved in managing some type of contract. Every time you get someone to perform a service you cannot, or don't want to do yourself, or buy a product that will enhance your current situation, you are entering the world of contract management.

On a general scale, a company's goods and services reflected in contractual form can account for 50-70% of its total costs. So contracts - and knowing how to manage them at work - is a critical competence of every manager.

Contracts don't have to mean 50-page bound documents that need to be written in legal language. Indeed, when presented with such a document most people go into 'freeze' mode. They make lots of assumptions and feel pressured to work in a transactional style of contract management, very much as a 'doer' rather than a negotiator/strategist. Many of us think contract management is about managing an agreed contract, but the 'supply chain' starts well before that. The whole thing starts when there is a need to source a contract, much before anything is put in writing. Indeed, it starts during the 'twinkle in the eye' of procurement.

This book is about becoming the optimal strategic contract manager … which starts long before any ink hits the page. We will go far beyond all the legal talk and ultimately focus on how to make the whole thing work, from go to woe - without too much woe. We will look at structures and strategies that will help you build flexible mechanisms into the contract process to ensure your agreement remains sustainable throughout the life of the contract - and that its effects are embedded as sustainable change … for good. A key focus of this book is the fact that, whether written or verbal, there are lots of changes along the way. Success is determined by how we manage those changes.

The underlying key to embedding sustainability into the contract management process is through the art of people management. Relationship planning and account management is not just the talk of marketers, it's the pointy end of contract management – as with many things it's all about who-you-know and how you relate to the people that matter.

The journey through this book will take you through the three pillars of Honig's Contract Management Model™ (the 'Contract Management Model'):

✓ Honig's Contract Management Lifecycle™ (the 'contract lifecycle')
✓ Honig's Leading Contract Management Model™ (the 'leading model'), consisting of:
  ➤ Contract Management Framework™ (the 'contract framework')
  ➤ Contract Management Methodology™, with templates (the 'contract methodology').

Enjoy the reading and then use the information, contract management wisdoms, tips and techniques to put yourself and your organisation in the driver's seat!

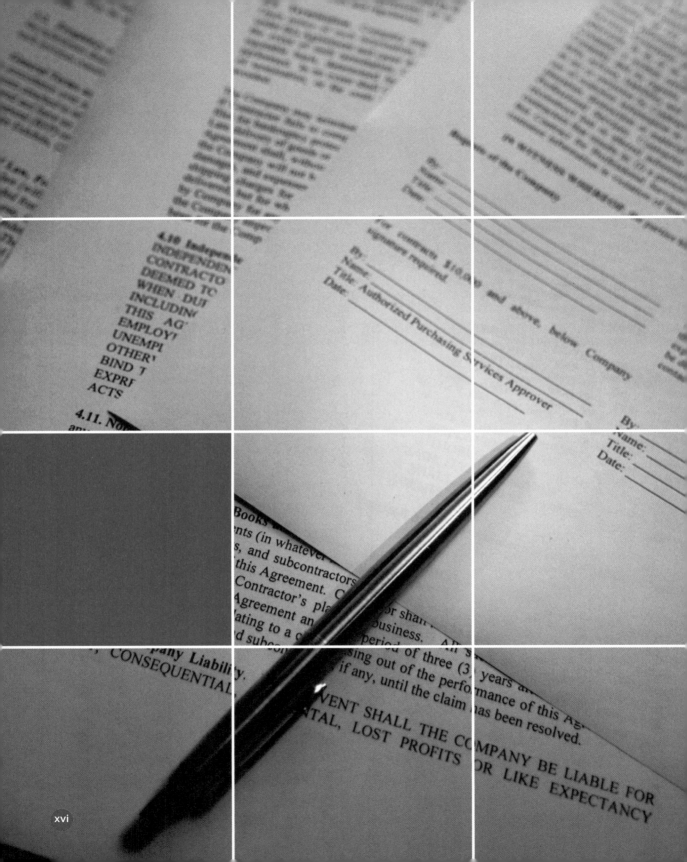

Planning Contracts

Chapter 1
The Contract Management Model

This chapter introduces the contract framework, from the front end of supply and procurement to the actual management of contracts. This framework is the missing link in the supply chain structure, and working within it will ensure things don't fall through the cracks. This is especially true in our modern work environment where managers tend to become specialists in one field, for example procurement or risk management, and leave, say, performance monitoring and payments to other areas within the organisation. Each manager needs to rise above their own area to see the bigger picture -- how each element of the supply chain can impact and influence the other to create a better outcome.

At this stage we introduce the contract management model, comprising a contract framework and a robust contract methodology, and pose questions about the importance of the contract and what having it in place should achieve. The contract framework structures the contract management lifecycle into four stages: plan, procure, manage and review (which includes vary and renew). It also demystifies terminologies, roles and responsibilities in the supply chain, which is step one in the 'accountability department'.

Everything has a lifecycle. With other, more structured disciplines, such as project management, managers are familiar with and are trained in the project management lifecycle. Until now, however, the contract management lifecycle hasn't featured as a structure, as contract management has generally been deemed a management skill that is learnt on the job.

We are all aware that we each have a lifecycle, from youth to adulthood and finally to old age. It's the way of the world. We expect things to start small, then blossom and finally to reach a crescendo. Many of us even take for granted why we are here and what our purpose is in life - we just get on with living. In the same way, contract managers just get on with managing. After all, that's what they are assigned to do, and that's what they do best.

However, it is true to say that the world of contracts also has a lifecycle of its own. It is often deemed to be organic, full of compromises and deal making. There's a lot of paperwork, handshakes and agreements, and much fuss with lawyers and accountants, especially when the contract has a great impact on our business, work life or quality of life. It's not often enough, though, that we take the time to sit back and analyse the 'food chain' of the contract management world: why it is needed, what the multiple purposes of its being are, and what are indeed the values and benefits it captures.

Contracts are such a significant part of our commercial landscape that we assume people know how the whole system works. With the whirlwind speed within which our global environment evolves, we often don't have the time to work out why a contract came to be because we are hustled into 'making it work', often with pressured timelines and cost restraints. It is this very frenetic behaviour that actually sets us back in time, through the inevitable need for rework (and the ensuing chaos) later down the track.

To start with, let's get a few terms straight in the name of consistency.

Firstly: when is a contract a contract?

Whenever there is **an agreement between two or more people**, where one person **offers** to give something to the other, and the other person accepts to **receive and compensate** the first, and where this exchange is **legally binding**, then you have a contract. In legal talk, there are four components:

➤ offer

➤ acceptance

➤ consideration

➤ legally enforceable agreement

Notice I didn't mention the word 'written'? That's because a contract can still be a contract even if it is verbal. With verbal contracts it's the 'legally enforceable' bit that may be a problem if things don't go exactly to plan, so it is better - and you are more protected - if the agreement is documented. (You also need to make sure that the document reflects reality and what was agreed - this will be discussed in detail later in Chapter 5.)

At this stage it is worth carefully defining 'contract management'. It's a fallacy that this term merely refers to the management of contracts, because this assumes that there is a contract in place. We won't make this assumption, because a lot goes on behind the scenes before the contract is created, written and signed.

Defining contract management

Firstly: when is a contract a contract?

A human analogy: planning 'Little Con'

We'll go right back to before the child is born, when its parents - in this case, Mr Needs and Ms Benefits - decided they wanted a child (let's call him 'Little Con'). They started by working out why indeed they wished for one or needed one, and discussed the benefits and whether having a child fitted into their lifestyle priorities. We will call this the design stage of Little Con. In essence, the lifecycle of Little Con started long before he was even born.

So Mr Needs and Ms Benefits worked out their long-term objectives (Stage One: The Plan) and then committed to having Little Con. But after much trying over a period of years, they saw they couldn't naturally *conceive Little Con so they decided to procure a child through an adoption agency (**Stage Two: The Procurement**).*

*After a protracted adoption period, where documents were signed and significant monies were paid (the 'consideration') based on their need to adopt a child under 6 months of age, Mr. Needs and Ms Benefits embarked on the third stage: the upbringing or 'management' of Little Con (**Stage Three: Manage**). Suddenly, they become parents of Little Con, not even aware of all the trials and tribulations he had undergone in his earlier life before they even procured him.*

*The final stage of Little Con's life (**Stage Four: Review**), incorporates the changes he goes through, how he grows and any introspection ('evaluate' in contract terms), until he is old enough to leave home and look after himself.*

The contract management lifecycle

One could say that the stages in the lifecycle of Little Con, represented above, going back to the time before he was conceived, or born, is akin to the lifecycle of contract management, as illustrated in the following diagram:

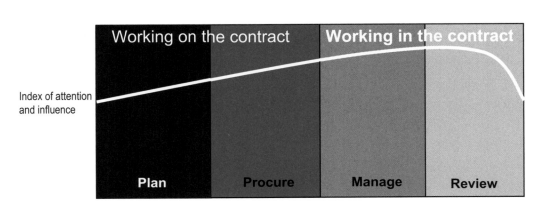

Figure 1: The 'Contract Management Lifecycle'.

We see in figure 1 that contract management is defined as starting with the planning of the contract, then working through the procurement, management and review stages systematically. In reality, this process is often managed in a piecemeal fashion, performed by various entities, or at worst in an ad-hoc manner with a transactional approach.

From this point on we are putting a structure to contract management to ensure future success. Structure the contract management process with embedded flexibility mechanisms and you will be enabled to manage it with a more streamlined approach.

This book takes us through the four lifecycle stages, allowing all managers in the sourcing supply chain – from procurement managers through to contract managers - to develop a structure for what has previously been at the very least a 'seat of the pants' approach or at the most a 'silo-based' strategy for this process. If there is no structure in the lifecycle we can very easily become rigidly bound by the power of the word, without building in mechanisms for flexibility along the way.

The four contract management phases can be consolidated into two philosophical modes of working: working on the contract and working in the contract.

Working on the contract

The first two stages of the contract management lifecycle – **planning** and **procuring** - are about working **ON** the contract, before it materialises. 'Contract' here is defined not in the material sense, ie not only as the words used to form the contract or the clauses inserted, although this is integral to the whole process. It is instead defined from the point of thinking about why you need an agreement at all, how and if you and your business will benefit from setting up a contract, and how the contract process - from

Working on the contract

7

accountability of roles to selection of provider – should be shaped up in order to create a successful outcome.

Someone, somewhere in your organisation (or your life) has been working on the contract management process at this front end. It may not be documented, it may or may not have been thought through very well or indeed explained, and it may have been at a board level or equally at a customer experience level.

In many organisations it is not usual that the contract manager (in the traditional sense of the title, the person who manages a contract already in existence) has full control of these two stages (plan, procure). Indeed, they may have been only superficially involved or informed about the basis of the plan and procure stages.

Either way, if a contract manager finds him/herself presented with a contract to manage, it is their fundamental responsibility to go back and examine the first two stages of the contract management lifecycle before he/she goes forward to managing the actual contract. In the absence of any clear instruction on stages one and two, it is their underlying responsibility to examine the realities of the situation by finding out the history and the facts.

Working in the contract management process

The third and fourth stages of the lifecycle – managing and reviewing – are about working IN the contract, once it is agreed. These stages assume that the first two stages of the lifecycle have been dealt with effectively and documented adequately.

By definition, entering stages three and four of the lifecycle presumes there is a contract in existence (whether verbal or in writing). However, without reference to structures set up in stages one and two, what could await the manager is a very rocky road paved with assumptions, guesswork, conjectures, notions or misbeliefs - and our businesses and livelihoods are too significant to risk working on guesswork.

Within the context setting of the lifecycle, we will discuss a structured framework within which we can work as contract managers: a robust framework that underpins the contract management lifecycle, one that offers practical tools, templates and techniques to help managers through the process. It's all part of structuring contract management for success.

The Four Powers of Contract Management

The contract lifecycle is embedded in the leading contract management model, which takes the four stages of the lifecycle and populates them with tools and techniques to arm you throughout the process.

> *You don't often see a poorly-structured contract succeed. You do see well-structured contracts poorly managed, with the result being pain on the way to achieving results. You also see badly-structured contracts well executed, with the result that the ultimate objective may still not be achieved.*

Our contract framework is the backbone to the lifecycle. It defines four main principles that give focus to each stage, and ultimately frame how to achieve meaningful contractual outcomes. They are:

Stage 1: Plan   <>   Principle 1: Clarity of Purpose
Stage 2: Procure   <>   Principle 2: Measurability
Stage 3: Manage   <>   Principle 3: Flexibility
Stage 4: Review   <>   Principle 4: Sustainability

This is illustrated in the following figure 2.

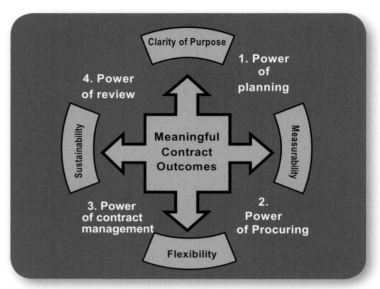

Figure 2: The 'four powers' model of contract management.

This 'four powers' model underpins the contract lifecycle and sets a very good structure for pacing through the four stages without missing links in the chain.

The four stages, with a view to achieving meaningful contract outcomes (i.e. benefits or objective realisation), are synonymous with four 'powers' (planning, procuring, managing and reviewing), each with their own unique set of tools, techniques and templates, which logically link together. The associated principles are critical success factors of the model.

Principle 1: Clarity of Purpose
There is an ultimate need to work out:

> ➤ why there is a contract in place in the first place (this is the need)
> ➤ why it is important, and

➤ what it is setting out to achieve (i.e. results, changes and benefits/ value adds, etc).

Principle 2: Measurability

You can't manage what you can't measure. So setting up performance standards which are measurable – both quantitatively and qualitatively – is really the only way you can monitor progress and results. This may sound obvious, but too many contracts are open-ended when it gets to measurability, leaving all parties out in the cold when things go awry.

Principle 3: Flexibility

One of the biggest risks in contract management is being inflexible. Building flexibility into the process as well as into the measurements is another key to success, especially at transition stages where there are new people taking over a contract or variations arise and need to be addressed.

Contracts that are overly prescriptive when it comes to things such as penalty-driven performance measurement, often end up stifling innovation and retarding otherwise achievable outcomes.

Principle 4: Sustainability

The fallacy with contracts is that when they come to the end of their term, their purpose is complete. The truth is the exact opposite: the effects of a contract can go on forever, because of benefits realised and changes that have been made. In light of sustainability, one needs to think long term.

For example, look at an executive search firm that headhunts senior executives, taking then from one senior position to another. Their contract is to source and place. However, the follow-up work (to investigate, for example, how successful the placement has been) is their knowledge management for the future. If they have placed a candidate in a role and that candidate is a bad fit or doesn't work out, the impact of the decision to place him is enormous.

The Four Powers of Contract Management

11

Chapter 1

Following up on client satisfaction after the contract term expires is checking on the sustainability of the outcomes. Decisions in contracts need to be made with this in mind, otherwise they could come back to haunt you. I have seen far too many transactional contract approaches, monitoring deliverables in a perfunctory manner, without thinking of future impacts, and only thinking of short term or operational results.

The four powers model comprises a sound set of principles which we will examine throughout the book. We will also examine how a contract manager manages both their suppliers and 'manages up' internally (see chapter 2) with work peers and superiors.

Contract management methodology

This is where a methodology template comes to good use. The methodology is simple and useable, making sure that each step of the way underpins the goal to *making contracts work.*

The methodology (see figure 3 opposite) is split into the four stages of contract management, aligning each stage to an outcome (benefit) and offering a series of relevant templates to work through the stages in a structured and systematic way. This methodology offers clarity of purpose, measurability, flexibility and reviewability.

The methodology has stood the test of time with procurement, auditors, accountants and lawyers. It's a risk management mitigation tool from a holistic perspective. The methodology can best be illustrated as follows.

Phases	Outcomes	Templates
PLAN	**Clarity of Purpose**	
Outline business case for proposed contract for management to formally endorse contract objectives	Fully endorsed in principle Contract scope aligned with business strategy	Contract Proposal Business Case EOI
PROCURE	**Measurability**	
Define all aspects of contract Ensure parties have a shared understanding of the why, what, how, who and when of the contract	Fully defined contract Endorsed terms & conditions Well transitioned contract Signed contract	Heads of Agreement Contract Mgmt Plan Transition Plan Contract/SLAs
MANAGE	**Flexibility**	
Undertake all planned activities in order to negotiate, communicate and performance manage the contract	Streamlined contract delivery Well managed outputs Well managed transition	Monitored KPIs Risk and issues log Relationship Management
REVIEW	**Sustainability**	
Monitor contract deliverables Review where appropriate Manage variations Publish lessons learnt for future contracts	Evaluated deliverables Risk/reward mechanisms applied Change of scope based on agreed variations (if any)	Variation report Evaluation Report

Figure 3: Contract management methodology template

Figure 3 shows a description of each of the stages and defines them by:

➤ relevance to the four powers framework;

➤ outcome;

➤ reference to relevant templates for each stage.

This is our roadmap for the rest of the book. It's your roadmap to success.

Each of the following chapters will deal with elements of the methodology, providing you with ideas, tips, templates and tools to help you cut down chaos and clear the path to accomplish your goals.

This structured approach will also help link the sourcing, procurement and contractual activities within your organisation.

Contract management methodology

Balance within the role of contract manager

So by now you might be thinking: 'Wait a minute! Is this book geared for the contract manager or procurement manager?' It's true to say that if a company structures these two roles separately, unless they work in tandem, the entire process remains exposed to transitional risk.

Transitional risk is common and exposes the contractual arrangement on a series of levels. The most obvious transition is moving between the four contract management phases, where things can fall through the cracks. For example, between the Procure and Manage stages. With both entities working together, the contract manager is better primed to address issues as they arise, and understand the true outcomes and objectives of the contract. In this way, the process is far more streamlined.

In order for the contract manager to be linked to the procurement process, a contract manager has to balance two sides of his/her role, as a Yin Yang approach. According to Chinese philosophy, Yin and Yang are complementary opposites as part of a greater whole. Everything has both Yin and Yang aspects, which constantly interact, never existing in absolute states. The Yin Yang of Contract Management comprises a balance between the sociocultural aspects (such as leading, problem solving and stakeholder management) against the technical side (such as terms and conditions, setting key performance indicators and performance monitoring, and scheduling). Figure 4 represents this balancing act.

Many traditional contract managers see themselves as technical, transactional and bound by the pages of the contract. There is another side to contracts however, and using the contract management fFramework, the sociocultural side of the contract manager is enabled.

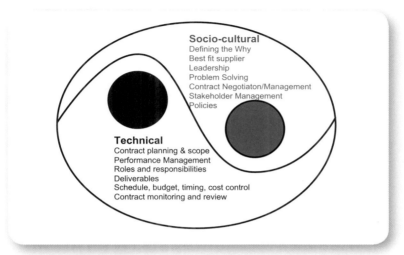

Socio-cultural
Defining the Why
Best fit supplier
Leadership
Problem Solving
Contract Negotiaton/Management
Stakeholder Management
Policies

Technical
Contract planning & scope
Performance Management
Roles and responsibilities
Deliverables
Schedule, budget, timing, cost control
Contract monitoring and review

Figure 4: The yin yang of contract management.

If the contract manager harnesses his/her influence throughout the entire process then true innovation can develop. The dual role of the contract manager takes on a higher purpose and links through to strategic procurement, thus creating a platform for **making contracts work**.

Roles and responsibilities

For governance purposes, the roles and responsibilities of each of the parties involved with the contract should be chartered and agreed amongst everyone involved in the process. A typical contract manager's role would look like this:

Responsibilities of a Contract Manager
➤ Develop the contract management plan
➤ Review periodically the contract management process (including the plan)
➤ Liaise between managers/users/suppliers to identify/resolve issues
➤ Meet regularly with contractor/s and key internal stakeholders re contract performance
➤ Monitor contractor's continuing performance against contract obligations

➤ Provide contractor with advice regarding developments within the department

➤ Provide accurate/timely reports to senior management, highlighting significant performance issues

➤ Provide adequate insurance terms throughout the contract period

➤ Ensure all products/services are certified to meet specs before supplier is paid

➤ Maintain adequate records in sufficient detail on an appropriate contract file

➤ Manage contract change procedures

➤ Resolve disputes as they arise

➤ Transition to new contract and/or provider

➤ Conduct post contract reviews

➤ Seek remedies in the event of contract breach; and report on all contracts

To complement the contract manager's role, use the following overall charter (Figure 5a, opposite) to map accountability and governance.

Governance embraces accountability and sound risk management. Whilst the roles and responsibilities opposite are not prescriptive, they can act as a guideline to the governance of contracts.

Procurement Manager
Tendering
Drafting of expression of interest
Drafting of request for tender or quote
Setting supplier selection criteria
Signing of heads of agreement
Drafting of heads of agreement
Outlining roles & responsibilities with expectations as to Key Performance Indicators (KPIs)
Setting performance definitions
Maintaining records of procurement
Contract Steering Committee (for large contracts)
Evaluating contract results (in terms of achievement of organisational objectives)
Approving variations
Endorsing transition plan
Scoring a contract management diagnostic profile based on critical success factors (Fig 18 Ch10)
Endorsing and approving status reports
Conflict resolution
Relationship management to ensure each parties have a shared understanding
Evaluating contract results (in terms of achievement of organisational objectives)
Supplier
Performing all deliverables in accordance with agreed Key Performance Indicators (KPIs)
Subcontractor monitoring and evaluation
Negotiating, communicating
Preparing status report
Transition plan

Figure 5a: Roles and responsibilities charter.

Roles and responsibilities

To truly manage a contract from beginning to end requires a collective set of management skills, illustrated in figure 5b, overleaf.

What is contract management?

Allocating
Adequate staff and resources to contract management

Reviewing
Contractor performance in terms of progress & compliance with contract provisions

Communicating with contractors to ensure maximum performance/ intended results

Approving and remitting payments in accordance with contract provisions and applicable law for acceptable work

Maintaining records of each contract that document activities such as procurement, management, and subcontractor monitoring, if applicable

Evaluating contract results in terms of the achievement of organisational objectives

Figure 5b: Contract management competencies.

Chapter 2
The Power of Planning
(the 'Why' of Contract Management)

This chapter deals with planning for the need to have a contract. It allows procurement managers to design the 'Why before how' rule, and to set out how a potential contractual need could align with business objectives and desired outcomes. It also sets the thinking straight for future risk planning and stakeholder management. It allows contract managers to ask the right questions (ie think like a procurement manager) and understand why they are doing what they are doing.

It allows all parties and management layers to define answers to the five 'why's'[1] of contract management, a step often otherwise assumed or deemed to be a luxury if time permits. It's about making contracts meaningful so they can be later managed artfully and within the intended purpose.

> *James O'Lachlin was a busy man. Before he even got to work in the morning, he had answered hundreds of text messages and emails, and attempted to put out many fires. So by the time he got to the office he was feeling stressed… and today was no exception. He arrived at his desk to find an unbound, unsigned draft copy of a contract with a covering note from his boss saying: 'Please get this work contracted out, we need the new technology platform in place by the end of this financial year, and time is running. Oh, and use the Compusystems mob, I owe them a favour…".*

---

1   Based on the Socratic method of asking why 5 times to get the root cause or underlying reason

Chapter 2

There was no note as to why the contract was needed, what level of service has been committed to, where or if there was a signed copy, and what the purpose of the contract was. Just another fine mess he was roped into.

But James was indeed a man of action, so he started by reading the piecemeal draft contract with all its handwritten amendments, slowly getting his head around it. After about an hour and a few very strong coffees, he felt ready to manage it. He felt he knew what the contract was there for and more or less understood the commercial terms and what they stood for. So he rang the contracted supplier named in the contract to arrange a meeting. James had no manual and no checklist of where to start. He started in the way he felt a responsible manager should, responding to his boss's request, knowing full well that his boss was never around to answer questions and, even if he was, he usually delegated all contract matters to him anyway.

But James's biggest mistake was that he felt he had to show he knew what he was doing. This meant assuming a lot that was left otherwise unsaid.

Many of us relate to James's dilemma in some shape or form. We all would like to know what we are doing and understand why we are doing it, and in the absence of strong communication we generally try to work out things for ourselves to fill in the gaps - after all, we have done it that way many times before, and it always works out in the end. Doesn't it?

Well, lets step back a minute, and be James's business coach. We will first get him to figure out the answers to a few questions.

The Philosophical 'Why'

James should firstly work out the philosophy behind the contract, making sure there are 'functional' reasons (see figure 6, p22) for contracting the services out. If, indeed, the reasons were classified in the 'dysfunctional' category (see figure 6, page 22), it still could mean the contract goes ahead, it just puts James in the powerful driver's seat of knowledge and information: the knowledge of his boss's plans for the company, and information about that particular area of the company.

The functional 'why' of contract management

The second 'why' is deeper and more complex. James has to find out a series of things to decipher the detailed reasons as to why the contract has arisen at this point, what major event or decision took place leading up to the contract, why it's important and what it's aiming to achieve. James knows that most of these things are unwritten, undocumented, and deep in his boss's head or buried in a handshake over a liquid lunch.

Managing Up

So it is up to James to MANAGE UP. It clearly is something that he needs to document so that he knows the origin or the source of the contract. Never mind that this would be going backwards in the contract management lifecycle, this is very common when communication doesn't happen as smoothly as it should. It's up to James to translate his understanding of the situation back to his boss in the most eloquent way possible to enable a structured, constructive conversation. In order to do so he has to spend a bit of time working out the 'why' of the contract.

The decision to contract out

The functional 'why' of contract management

The first rule of contracts: 'why' the contract is needed

There are two types of 'why' or reasons as to why people contract out. The first is the 'philosophical why', which we can map out according to the following diagram:

	Economics	Expertise
Functional Reasons	Scale	Specialty
Dysfunctional Reasons	Sale	Surrender

Figure 6: The philosophical 'why' of the contract using the four 'S' outsourcing model.

This model[1] divides the 'why' of the contract into functional and dysfunctional reasons. Needless to say, we would like our contracts to fit into the 'functional' category. We would like to or are often led to believe that this is indeed the case.

However, being realistic about the reasons behind each contract we manage will bring a level of transparency to every commercial relationship that is at the very least refreshing, and quite possibly enlightening and enabling for the people involved.

The functional reasons for outsourcing or out-tasking are sound and smart:

Four Philosophical reasons for contracting out

> ➤ **Scale:** Accessing economies of scale and efficiencies that an organisation cannot achieve with its own skills and resources. It's often more cost efficient to use external services' larger scale buying power or other cost advantages.

---

1   Coined by M. Zucchini, previously CIO of Fleet/Norstar

➤ **Specialty:** Accessing specialised expertise that would be too expensive to hire inhouse as an ongoing staff overhead. This means, either you don't have (or don't want to invest in) the specialty skills to efficiently and effectively resource the contract, and/or find it smarter to get another person or company to perform the work rather than reinventing the wheel in-house, given time and budget restraints.

The dysfunctional reasons for outsourcing or out-tasking are often driven by shorter-term goals.

If your contract falls into the 'dysfunctional' categories for outsourcing or out-tasking (see figure 6 opposite), then often the 'smarts' of the exercise are lost and shorter term goals tend to drive the need. These shorter-term reasons usually become the drivers when there is a need to cash up, a lack of time or knowledge to think things through, or an unwillingness to scope the contract internally due to 'surrendering' this exercise to the provider. The two dysfunctional categories resulting from this phenomenon are coined as:

➤ **Sale:** Turning non-productive assets of capital and IT equipment into cash to improve a balance sheet and reduce a headcount.

➤ **Surrender:** Simplifying an agenda by essentially giving up and hoping that a contract for service yields the outcomes that the company/manager desires.

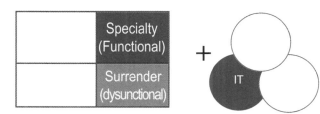

The contract was drafted because of a need for specialty skill-resourcing reasons but also with a dysfunctional approach to 'hope for the best' with the provider. This is due to the fact that the contract was about out-tasking technological services which he knew very little about.

Figure 6a:

The first rule of contracts: 'why' the contract is needed

So, going back to James O'Lachlin's dilemma at the beginning of this chapter, after listening to our coaching he decided to start sorting out the reasons for the contract by using the two tools above – the philosophical 'why' and the functional 'why'.

Based on his knowledge of the company and the way his boss works, and some further investigation, he framed the reasons as follows:

1. Specialty (a functional 'why')

2. Surrender (a dysfunctional 'why')

3. Technological (a functional 'why')

James had worked out that the reasons for drafting the contract are mainly functional (specialty skill-resourcing by out-tasking technological services) but there is an element of dysfunction in the contract because the technological services he was out-tasking were something he knew very little about. From this analysis James understood that there was a dysfunctional philosophical issue in the style that the contract was drafted, basically leaving it very open-ended and generic in a 'hope for the best' approach.

However, it also became clear that there was a need to outsource the services to a specialist company who had the knowledge and expertise to handle the contract. This is not an uncommon analysis when dealing with technical services-related contracts, where subject matter experts are needed for their knowledge and know-how.

One of James' biggest known risks now is established, being the generality of the contract and the 'hope for the best' approach.

James needs to step back to the stage where the contract was designed and planned, and write his version of the scenario for his boss to acknowledge (the enactment of 'Managing Up'). In order to do this we will arm him with our first template in the planning stage – the contract proposal.

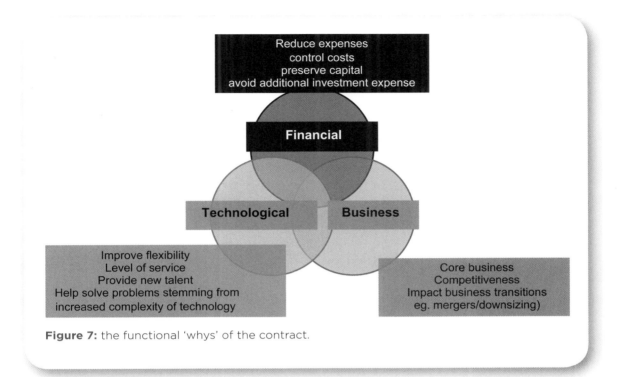

Figure 7: the functional 'whys' of the contract.

The second rule of contracts: business functionality

The second type of 'why' or raison d'etre of the contract refers to business functionality.

Apart from the philosophical reasons driving the creation of the contract as set out in figure 6 (see page 22), the decision to contract out can be driven from, and impacts a wide variety of needs, in particular three core functions in an organisation: financial, business and technological, as displayed in figure 7.

Now that James has the background straight – where the idea came from and what the contract is setting out to achieve – he needs to start structuring the first stage of the contract management framework: **Formulating a Contract Proposal.**

You may be thinking that the horse has already bolted – after all, a draft contract sits on his desk. However, by 'bolting with the horse', the race is lost. James needs to reign in the horse, or in this case the contract management lifecycle, to get a grip of what's going on.

It's true to say that a well-executed contract with no structure to the process is a recipe for disaster.

This structures the science of contract management, because it sets out processes and standards for future negotiation and variations. It also cements and embeds the needs analysis right at the very start, while setting up a flexible mechanism to allow for variations in the name of progress and improvement. Thus, change management becomes progress management, leaving behind ad hoc, laisser-faire management.

CONTRACT PROPOSAL FORM	
Section	**Questions to be answered**
Background	Why has the contract arisen now?
	Major event/decision leading to contract?
	Problem to address or opportunity to exploit?
Alignment with our Priorities	How does the contract align with commercial priorities & strategies?
Objectives	Why is the contract important?
	What is it aiming to achieve?
Key Contract Outcomes (Benefits)	What long-term changes will result?
	What financial benefits will result?
	What operational improvements will result?
	What benefits or 'value add' will result from the contract?
Key Contract Outputs (Deliverables)	What tangible products/services are produced by the contract?
	What form will these products/services take?
	What will the contract deliver to the client?
Contract Scope	What are the key deliverables?
	What items are out of scope?
Research and Evidence	Evidence that justifies contract?
	Evidence that contract will achieve desired outcomes?
	What similar contracts have been conducted for lessons learnt?
Contract Risks	Major risks in delivering the contract? Plans to mitigate such risks?
Stakeholders	Who are the parties to the contract?
	Who are the people most affected by the contract?
Term	Date for commencement.
	Date for completion.
	Date for reviews.
	Any milestones?
Budget and Resources	What budget is required?
	What resources (people, equipment, systems) are required?

Template 1: Contract proposal form

Contract proposal form

Stage One: ("Plan")

James examined phase one of our contract management methodology:

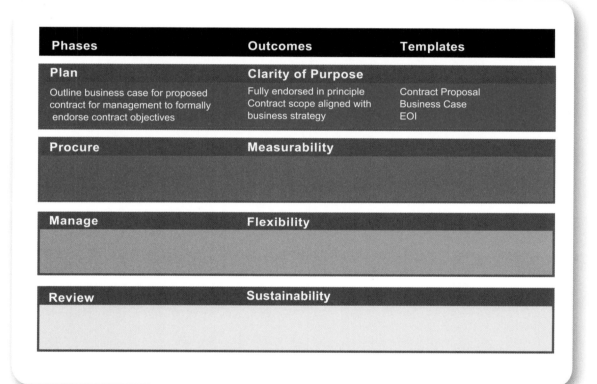

Figure 8: Contract management methodology phase one.

…and structured the process by writing out a contract proposal form (template 1) and model template of which follows (case study #1 on page 36).

James realised that the value of this exercise is in asking the right set of questions. If these questions are not understood by the contract manager, or if there is no shared understanding between the procurement head and the contract manager, then we enter the area of assumptions, which is very risky territory. Never enter into the area of assumptions, iron these out before you start. That's what the contract proposal is about.

Expression of interest

Following the formulation of a Contract Proposal, a market investigation process can be managed using a formal Expression of Interest (EOI). An (EOI) provides a starting point in the overall procurement process. Commonly, government agencies publish EOI documents to attract and short-list potential bidders.

The EOI is an optional phase in the tendering process. This allows prospective bidders to acknowledge their interest in the procurement document and begin a dialogue with the client.

Using this process, it would have allowed James (or his boss, if he had been that way inclined) to explore market intelligence and know-how, current suppliers and what competitors are doing in this space.

An EOI step would usually only be employed for significant scale projects, but it does allow a company to do sound research on the potential market and contract before embarking on it. A classic EOI would:

- ✓ invite prospective consultants or contractors to make submissions
- ✓ enable contractors and vendors to state their ability to meet specific project requirements, either individually or by combining their abilities
- ✓ enable contractors and vendors to be assessed for inclusion or otherwise in a short list for invitation to submit a consultancy proposal or a tender

Stage One: ("Plan")

James found that an EOI process had not been carried out in any formal manner, or indeed at all. It certainly wasn't his boss's style.

Bracing himself, he decided to confront his boss with a fully documented contract proposal. Knocking sharply on the door with full apparent confidence, he found the office empty. His PA said he would be back in 10 days, he had some urgent overseas business to attend to. Some things never change....

Case Study #1:
Clarity of Purpose
"As clear as crystal...or mud?"

The business problem

Telco Ltd. was about to enter a contract for an integrated billing system that would radically change the way it managed its billing process, including customer charging, complaints and database management. Such a contract was at the core of its business, because any kinks in the process could mean losses in the millions. Its current billing system had significant problems that not only led to major losses in incorrect charging, but also meant millions of manpower hours lost or wasted in fixing the problems and additional revenue losses in compensating disgruntled customers.

The first business problem was that Telco Ltd began as a monopoly, so accurate invoicing wasn't a high level priority. Its underlying philosophy for many years had been that, if it could not provide an accurate invoice, what was a customer going to do, switch to another provider? The previous Telco CEO had been quoted as defending its billing system by saying '...it's as good as any of our competitors!'.

Secondly, its billing systems were designed years ago, when it was still a monopoly. With the growing number of telecommunications sellers now presenting to the market, customer perception was suddenly of critical importance. Switching to another telecommunications supplier was no longer as hard as it used to be...

Telco Ltd's systems were not designed to handle the diversity and agility of services required today. Up until now Telco had not been ready to invest in the overhaul of its billing systems, especially while its customers were willing to allocate their own resources or hire someone from the growing 'cottage industry' to find and fix billing mistakes.

This cottage industry consisted of service providers who fed off inaccuracies within the system and claimed to significantly lower company's telecommunications spending through overcharge recovery, guaranteeing they would find errors in billing from telecommunications providers and generate overcharge recoveries that could amount to tens of thousands of dollars. They also offered to review telecommunications contract agreements to eliminate hidden costs and overcharge processes before they happened.

A challenge arose within Telco Ltd when they found that there was no one in their company with the technical skills to write the brief for a new billing system, so after countless workshops and management forums, it was decided that they would get a consultant firm to do this.

The consultant brief

The consultants who were hired to write the brief for the billing service contract were briefed through Telco Ltd's operations department. As a result, they didn't spend enough time getting to the bottom of the problem, or understanding the real need for the change. All they understood was that a system was required to be built to deliver an all-in-one platform for order management, integrated provisioning, convergent billing, CRM, customer and agent web portals, reporting, trouble ticketing, IVR, equipment inventory plus much more. They believed that if Telco Ltd put its operations on autopilot, it could focus on winning customers and generating revenue. Indeed, that's how the consultant brief was framed.

A couple of major conditions were overlooked in the brief -- they were assumed to be understood, but not put into writing. The first was the need to satisfy customer demand for billing accuracy and obliterate the cottage industry that underpinned the perception of inaccuracy. It wasn't enough for Telco Ltd to build an accurate system. It also needed a management process that demystified it and re-educated customers, eradicated preconceptions of inaccuracy and also handled customer queries with a user-friendly, transparent approach.

The second assumption was that the support and maintenance of the new billing system was to be a separate contract, not linked to the design and provision of the actual system.

Both these unfounded assumptions led to weaknesses in the contract brief and ensuing contract, which in turn threatened the viability of the contract.

What eventuated

The brief was written to take into account the billing system needs, and was written to technical perfection. The challenge, according to Telco Ltd, was to find and select the best-fit service provider that had the systems (but not necessarily the support services) to underpin system management and maintenance.

The reality was that the system was built (based on a design, test and build contract) with no reference to maintenance or support of the system immediately thereafter. In actual fact, a separate contract for maintenance and support of the system was drawn up and agreed with a separate service provider, different to the provider of the billing system itself.

Telco Ltd focused much of its energy on the output of the billing system, and less on the outcomes. Two very powerful outcomes that were not outlined in the brief were:

1) The re-education of customer perception, measured by customer complaints and customer release/loss rates.

2) Alignment with Telco Ltd's business priorities, one of which was to ensure all systems were maintained and supported by the service provider of the system (unless a business case could be put forward to justify deviation from this priority). The underlying reason for this priority was to ensure streamlined management processes that negate fault allocation between service providers and also that accountability for design and implementation was inextricably linked.

Results

When measuring the impact of the new system once installed, it was discovered that billing accuracy over the first 12 months had increased by 12%, but customer complaints had increased by 2%. The increase of customer complaints came as a shock to board members, who discovered that the increase was partly due to system support issues and partly due to a proliferation of billing experts checking for errors, knowing that new systems always have teething problems and so capitalising on this perceived inherent weakness, influencing customers with scare tactic promotions.

After a period of 24 months had passed post installation, performance measurement of the system unearthed a 38% increase in accuracy, but a 12% increase in customer billing complaints based on issues largely related to system support and maintenance.

Questions

1. If the consultants (who wrote the brief) completed a contract proposal form (see Template 1, page...), how would the circumstances and outcomes have changed?

2. Would the contract and its manifestations been any different?

3. What issues could have been saved had they done this?

4. Use the contract proposal form in Template 1 to sort out solutions, acting as if you were the manager at Telco Ltd who was charged to commission the brief. Then take a look at the model answer following, and carry out a discussion with your work colleagues to compare and contrast your thoughts.

If you could rewind the clock (by two years), the Telco Ltd manager could have briefed the consultant writing the brief to the billing provider using the following contract proposal form:

Contract Proposal Form

Section	Questions to be answered before consultant is commissioned to write brief
Background	**_Why has the contract arisen now?_** The contract has arisen now because there are an increasing number of inaccuracies in Telco Ltd's billing systems, leading to a record number of customer complaints for reimbursements and an equally unprecedented loss of customers (primarily to its biggest rival, Oclet Ltd.) , and an unparalleled waste of manpower to fix avoidable problems. **_Major event/decision leading to contract?_** A major event leading to the contract being commissioned has been the deregulation of the telecommunications industry, breaking the monopoly stranglehold that Telco Ltd had on its customers and opening the floodgates to multiple rival service providers. A decision was made to set up a performance management regime for all Telco Managers, including a KPI to measure the number of customer complaints and customer losses relating to each of their respective divisions. Data relating to billing complaints and resultant customer losses within each business division became a priority target to the board, as it was revealed that 59% of customer complaints concerned customer billing errors. **_Problem to address or opportunity to exploit?_** The problem to address is the lack of integration in the multiple billing systems in the company, and customer perception that such errors made up a large part of Telco's profit margins. The opportunities include radically changing the way Telco Ltd manages its billing process, also using it as a customer relationship management tool as well as a management indicator of executive performance.

Contract Proposal Form

Alignment with our Priorities	***How does the contract align with commercial priorities & strategies?*** The contract aligns with Telco Ltd's commercial priorities and strategies given the immediate imperative to gain a competitive advantage post deregulation, and a wish to retain and grow its customer base. Underlying this is the need to reeducate its customers on how the new billing system will improve accuracy and how it will work for the customer. Customer satisfaction is the priority at all times, as with satisfied customers the company will gain a competitive advantage. New manager KPIs revolve around customer satisfaction, retention and attraction at all levels. Company policy insists on all major service providers providing systems to also maintain and support the system as part of the contract.
Objectives	***Why is the contract important?*** The contract is important because Telco Ltd needs to improve its customer perception of customer-friendly systems and transparent, efficient and effective services, including its core system of billing. Billing is at the heart of Telco's systems because it encompasses an ability to track and manage customer relationships ***What is it aiming to achieve?*** The contract is aiming to achieve: • increased customer retention, loyalty and satisfaction; • reduced complaints about billing; • a renewed customer perception that Telco Ltd is the preeminent service provider of services related to voice, data and cellular phones.
Key Contract Outcomes (Benefits)	***What long-term changes will result?*** Increased customer retention rates by X%. ***What financial benefits will result?*** Cost savings of $X million ***What operational improvements will result?*** Cost savings of $X million ***What benefits or 'value add' will result from the contract?*** Customer relationship management that would allow even further loyalty and customer satisfaction without the 'auto-pilot' factor impacting on personal relationships with customer.

Contract Proposal Form

Chapter 2

Contract Proposal Form

Key Contract Outputs (Deliverables)	*What tangible products/services are produced by the contract?* *What form will these products/services take?* *What will the contract deliver to the client?* Products/services produced by the contract will include an all-in-one platform for order management, integrated provisioning, customer relationship management, convergent billing, customer and agent web portals, reporting, trouble ticketing, IVR, equipment inventory and full support and maintenance of the system.
Contract Scope	*What are the key deliverables?* The key deliverables include full system design, test, build and maintenance. *What items are out of scope?* Items out of scope include customer interfacing with regards to reeducating the customer and change management (internal and external)
Research and Evidence	*Evidence that justifies contract?* Evidence that justifies the contract includes data that reveals increased customer loss and customer perception of exploitation and billing inaccuracies. *Evidence that contract will achieve desired outcomes?* Evidence that the contract will achieve its desired outcomes includes an overseas company, Tezeq Co, having used the provider and vouched for its successful implementation. *What similar contracts have been conducted for lessons learnt?* The only other similar contracts within Telco Ltd to learn lessons from are the outsourcing of our call centre contract, which was riddled with issues and from which we are learning (see project evaluation report AG325132 in archives).

Contract Proposal Form

Contract Risks	*Major risks in delivering the contract?* Major risks in delivering the service provider contract include: • consultant not fully understanding Telco Ltdneeds and priorities, • system not designed to sufficiently interface with Telco's standard operating environment, • system not properly supported or maintained once installed, • timelines not being met, • competitors building better systems faster . Other medium to long-term risks include change management not managed properly (internal/external stakeholders).
Stakeholders	*Who are the parties to the contract?* The parties to the contract are Telco Ltd and ITD Pty Ltd who have been commissioned to write the brief to the service providers (to be selected) *Who are the people most affected by the contract?* The people most affected/impacted by the contract (major stakeholders) include Telco Ltd, ITD Pty Ltd, the heads of all business divisions, the board, shareholders and customer groups.
Term	*Date for commencement*: 10th March this year *Date for completion:* 10th October this year *Date for reviews:* Monthly *Milestones:* as set in the service level agreement
Budget and Resources	What budget is required? $X What resources (people, equipment, systems) are required? as detailed in service level agreement

Template 1a: Telco Ltd's draft contract proposal form.

Procurement & Outsourcing

Chapter 3
The Power of Strategic Procurement

Within the contract framework, this chapter deals with strategic procurement and its ramifications. It elaborates on a strategic procurement plan, guidelines and definitions. Once this scene is set, the book discusses the value of sound contract management planning, an exercise that is ideally worked out between the procurers and the managers. It demonstrates how to define clarity of purpose, and the fundamental requirements of the contract.

This is the science of contract management, partly because it sets out processes and standards for future negotiation and variations. It also cements and embeds the needs right at the start while setting up a flexibility mechanism to allow for variations in the name of progress and improvement. Thus, change management becomes progress management.

We also examine purchasing types, such as tendering, request for quotes and the need for governance in the selection process. Definitions of outsourcing, out-tasking and offshoring are explored, and in doing so, we examine the 'value for money' conundrum, offering a 'value for money' checklist that is useful to all managers.

James took the situation into his own hands and started to think like an accountable business owner. He decided to document the procurement

> *stage of the process, to get a grip on the situation and attempt to find clarity in what had transpired.*
>
> *However, James wasn't quite sure how to handle this. Especially since he had highlighted that one of the biggest risks in the proposal stage was not selecting the best fit supplier for the job.*
>
> *In addition to this, given his boss's preference for this particular supplier with whom he'd lunch with several times a month, he felt he had his hands tied somewhat; but being a man of process, he was determined to think through the logics of procurement even though procurement was to all intents and purposes 'dealt with'. James really wanted to add value to the process.*

Defining strategic procurement

James needs to start thinking strategically, with a 'procurement hat' on. Strategic procurement is about putting together long-term plans for the timely supply of goods/services that tie in with your business goals. It is now seen as vital to competitiveness and has a significant impact on financial performance.

Procurement issues

As his business coach, I would tell James that, in the procurement/acquisition cycle, if planning and purchasing is done strategically, the administration and management of contracts become so much easier.

There are many issues relevant to the procurement stage. These include setting up and following:

Procurement policies

1. Procurement policy, guidelines and definitions
2. Processes to select the best fit supplier
3. Mechanisms to measure supplier performance

James searched the office files and finally put his hand to a rather dated procurement policy. From this he gathered information on what the boundaries were in terms of seeking and securing suppliers, covering things like:

✓   *How to select suppliers;*
✓   *Compliance with legislation and risk standards;*
✓   *How to make the most of buying power;*
✓   *Securing competitive advantage whilst protecting the organisation;*
✓   *Best value for money and corporate responsibilities.*

Selecting the best-fit supplier

Selecting the best-fit supplier was and is the most pressing issue to deal with for James, and indeed for all procurement/contract managers. The focus here should be to **select suppliers that are aligned with your business values and culture and can communicate well with your existing staff.**

Remember, suppliers become part of the corporate 'extended family'. It's true to say (although a very dismal thought), that we spend more waking hours with our colleagues at work, than we do with our family at home. The longer the business relationship is to last, the more important is the stage where foundations are laid and set.

Identifying 'best-fit' is a multi-dimensional exercise, best represented by this best-fit scorecard using a two pronged approach:

Scorecard	
The Business Fit	**The People Management Fit**

Engagement scope and objectives
• Competitive quality and performance guarantees
• Flexibility and initiative methods/systems for:
    - Sustainability of best practice
    - Accurate billing and reporting
	Ability to meet business challenges
	• Proven verifiable track records (customer references)
	• Selection of experienced subcontractors
	• Ability to service 'service level agreement'

Comparable business drivers	
Compliance with regulations, quality assurance	Resource plan with sufficient resources
Resource strategy showing optimal use of people, finances and equipment	Compatible business and people cultures Relationship model (policies, procedures)
Workload and priorities	Account management (including management quality and depth)
Database management	Succession plans for key people
Workflow processes	Transition plan
No conflicts re vendor licenses/existing contracts	Resource planning and firewalling between accounts
Ability to meet industry standards	Technology know how and shared understandings
Existing infrastructure: • financial stability • core business, size, geographic coverage	Cost savings and performance improvements

Template 2: Best-fit scorecard to identify best fit on all levels

James needs to go through the best-fit scorecard on previous page, and check off and evaluate the capabilities against three different companies to see who would score the highest. In Template 2, there are 10 business-related criteria, and 10 people-related criteria. The 'fit' score (out of 20) should ideally have balanced scores in both business-related criteria, and people-related criteria. When James is doing market research and evaluating best-fit suppliers, he should be sure to investigate on all these grounds. There may occasionally be justifiable reasons for selecting an incumbent who doesn't have the best-fit score, but this exercise requires such justification before proceeding with procurement.

After James uses the overall scorecard to assess best fit, he then evaluates the best-fitting companies with some or all of the criteria that align with his company's business objectives, according to its business plan.

Whilst we are in the throws of defining things, we must also at this stage define the differences between outsourcing, out-tasking and offshoring. It's important to understand these differences so that we can categorise our contracts and then relationship map accordingly (see Chapter 4). 'Contracting out' is layman terminology for either outsourcing or out-tasking.

Define: outsourcing vs out-tasking

At this point, it is essential to work out what is being contracted out: is it an entire process/production, or is it only certain parts of a work process? The answer to this question differentiates outsourcing (holus bolus) from out-tasking parts of the services. This differentiation helps inform how the contract should be formed and also how to apply the philosophical 'why' of the contract to the situation at hand.

Outsourcing defined, is 'hiring out' an entire work process – individual tasks and all. An example would be to 'process incoming emails'.

Selecting the best-fit supplier

Out-tasking defined, is 'hiring out' small tasks of an entire work process. People who hire out individual 'parts' of a job, 'out-task'. Out-tasking is usually done on a smaller scale and for a shorter period.

A one-time project would usually be considered out-tasking rather than outsourcing. Out-tasking doesn't dictate how a job should be done – it only dictates what should be done. An example would be to 'Forward incoming emails to James@acme.com'. In all these circumstances, the responsibilities for the risk are being shifted to some other person(s) or company(s), given their expertise or resources.

Offshoring is a type of outsourcing that involves the relocation by a company of a business process from one country to another; typically an operational process, such as manufacturing, or supporting processes, such as accounting. The economic logic is to reduce costs. If some people can use some of their skills more cheaply than others, those people have the comparative advantage. The idea is that countries should freely trade the items that cost the least for them to produce.

Value-for-money equation

The decision whether to outsource, out-task or outsource offshore is critical to a company's overall performance.

The reason behind the choice of supplier should be based on a series of equations or formulas, the most fundamental of which is the **value-for-money equation**. It is equivalent to the return on investment in the financial world. It is the ultimate decider when choosing your business partner/supplier.

The **value-for-money equation** is not only about cost or price. It is about the weight of value the supplier brings to your company. The equation is based on four main elements:

1. **Characteristics and capabilities of the supplier** (legal, financial, technical, experience and qualifications, reputation, cultural fit)
2. **Characteristics of the offer** (meeting specifications, fitness for purpose, compliance, scope for value management, sustainability, conformity to deliverables and terms)
3. **Whole-of-life costs** (price, cost containment, maintenance costs, etc)
4. **Strategic and marketplace considerations** (relationship value, market structure, length of supply chain and its vulnerability to disruption, effect on future requirements, potential for development)

The value-for-money equation looks like this:

Value for Money = Capabilities + Offer + WOL Costs + Marketplace

The above scorecard is a user-friendly approach to assess potential suppliers. Many companies and government agencies have a financial and risk threshold, at which point their procurement policy requires them to enter into a tendering situation.

Tendering was created to put fairness into the value-for-money decision. When a contract exceeds a set amount (usually over $50,000 or $100,000, depending on the company) that company may decide to set out the general terms of the contract and submit it to a few selected parties (selective tender) or to the world at large (public tender).

Value-for-money equation

Tenders

49

A tender is characteristically a binding contract to supply goods and services for a price, and usually includes:

✓ receiving formal written offers, either by public or selective process;

✓ evaluating responses ;

✓ choosing one provider from amongst the tenders/bidders.

When is a tender not a tender? An expression of interest (see Chapter 1) is not a tender. Indeed, no organisation is obliged to follow this process with a tender process, even if expectations are that they would.

Tenders are more common in government agencies, but constitute due process for formal and fair evaluation of market players and their capabilities. The tender process underpins the entire philosophy for value for money (a concept discussed above and at the beginning of chapter 4).

Compliance

Compliance means adhering to certain standards, which could include health and safety, legal, regulatory and risk standards. Compliance is often a first and foremost measure in a contract, often linked to sanctions or penalties for non-compliance.

Making the most of buying power

One must be very careful when placing a high penalty of non-compliance with any of the above matters, as compliance is really non-negotiable. Whilst some areas of compliance have tolerance levels associated with them, others don't (such as safety). Make sure you do the groundwork and obtain legal and commercial advice relating to all such matters.

Procurement policies are in place to achieve functional advantages (see figure 6 in Chapter 2, the 4 'S' model), such as economies of scale or specialist expertise. Procurement guidelines take into account the philosophical advantages for outsourcing/out-tasking, as referred to in Chapter 2.

On the flip side of buying power advantages, and in line with gaining competitive advantages, all procurement decisions should be mindful of risk management and protect their organisation from exposure to risk when sourcing external assistance.

It is at the procurement stage that mechanisms need to be established to measure supplier performance. This will set the ground rules for performance monitoring in the third stage of contract management – the 'Manage' phase.

Mechanisms for measurement of supplier performance should focus on outcomes and outputs.

Outcomes are the **'why', the benefits** resulting out of the contract (plus any value add that the contract brings through innovation), for example, improved efficiencies or more time to focus on strategic planning.

Outputs are **'what'** is being delivered. Measurables should focus on achieving the outcomes through performing the outputs, for example, the new building or the completed report or the delivered survey.

When setting up the contract, the anticipated and agreed benefits – or outcomes - should appear in the introductory 'Recitals' section. The outputs, or deliverables, usually are spelled out in detail in the body of the contract and with service contracts often form part of a more detailed specification called 'Service Level Agreements' (SLA's').

Stage Two ("Procure")

At this stage, James should be looking at setting up a structure for the procurement stage of the framework. Let's look at our template methodology for stage two ('Procure'):

Phases	Outcomes	Templates
Plan	**Clarity of Purpose**	
Procure	**Measurability**	
Define all aspects of contract Ensure parties have a shared understanding of the why, what, how, who and when of the contract	Fully defined contract Endorsed terms & conditions Well transitioned contract Signed contract	Heads of Agreement Contract Mgmt Plan Transition Plan Contract/SLAs
Manage	**Flexibility**	
Review	**Sustainability**	

Figure 3b: contract management methodology phase two.

Although James has been presented with a draft form of contract from his boss, he may do well to refrain from using this. Starting afresh will ensure the contract is not tied in to legacy clauses and will ensure that no vital part of the new agreement falls between the cracks.

At this stage, ensuring all the parties to the contract have a shared understanding of the 'why-what-how-who and when' of the contract is critical.

I would coach James to start defining all aspects of the contract in a simple, easy-to-read form, which he can use to discuss with suppliers, and then to instruct lawyers to draft the contract. James would do well to start putting together a 'heads of agreement'.

A Heads of Agreement is a non-binding document outlining the main issues relevant to a tentative (partnership or other) agreement or contract. It allows parties to state, in their own words, what they believe the contractual agreement will involve, in laymen's terms. The best approach is for each party to draft their own version and then to share this together and have a joint heads of agreement written up prior to any contract being signed. This will iron out misunderstandings, leading to a shared understanding between the parties. It will also be a clear roadmap and set of instructions for lawyers to draft the contract.

Heads of Agreement

Many parties to a contract skip this stage. There is no particular template for this, but the heads of agreement usually spells out the names of the parties, the term, what it sets out to achieve, basic roles and responsibilities and main deliverables. The wording should be in Plain English and is usually informal.

Contract management plan

To ensure sound procurement management is in place, James should fill out a contract management plan. For effective business contract management, it is recommended that every contract manager plans for the contract management process prior to its commencement. Preparing such a plan streamlines the administration and review of service contract performance in terms of:

- ✓ efficiency;
- ✓ cost effectiveness;
- ✓ service provider accountability;
- ✓ results

A contract management plan contains all the key information about how a contract will be managed. It establishes systems and processes to ensure

Contract management plan

that the contractor complies with the terms and conditions during the performance of the contract. It also enables the contract manager to:

✓ develop a good understanding of the contract, and the responsibilities of the parties involved; and

✓ establish a system against which the performance of both parties can be monitored and problems can be identified early - either before or as they occur.

The contract management plan is a living document. Its development should commence during the procurement planning stage, and it should be reviewed and updated throughout the procurement process and the life of the contract, particularly in the event of any change or variation taking place.

At the procurement planning stage, consideration needs to be given to:

✓ who will manage the contract
✓ how the contractor's performance will be monitored
✓ what the risks associated with the contract are, and how they will be managed during the course of the contract, and
✓ what reporting requirements will be required of the contractor
✓ performance measures to be used
✓ milestones and reporting requirements, and
✓ implementation / transitional issues

At the beginning of the contract management phase, just about where James is positioned now, the contract manager should finalise the contract management plan, by identifying the critical clauses in the contract and other requirements that may influence the management of the contract.

Chapter 3

CONTRACT MANAGEMENT PLAN

Which: Description of Contract
- ✓ Key parties
- ✓ Expected outcomes and objectives
- ✓ Key deliverables: brief description of the work to be performed.
- ✓ Reporting requirements & milestones for critical events

What: Positions and Structure and Performance Definitions
- ✓ Specific staff positions, resources and structure to be assigned to contract management;
- ✓ Performance management: how the contract management staff will review and supervise contractor performance, progress, and contract compliance
  - ➤ Staff training

How: Contract Management Processes
- ✓ Accountability, results, and positive programmatic impact from service contracts
- ✓ Risk management and mitigation strategies
- ✓ Transitions (in and out, detailing impacts on stakeholders and key documents required)
- ✓ Conflict and disputes resolutions
- ✓ Contract variations handling (non-compliance, under performance)
- ✓ Payment conditions and terms
- ✓ Contract management evaluation, having responsibility for:
  - ➤ each service contracted
  - ➤ internal controls, financial integrity, and internal audit
  - ➤ performance standards set

Template 3: The contract management plan.

Contract management plan

Transition planning

One of the biggest risks in contract management is transition. There are several levels of transition in a contract period, including:

- ✓ Transitioning into a new contract from:
  - ➤ services previously handled in-house
  - ➤ a previous provider
  - ➤ a renewed contract based on revised terms
- ✓ Transitioning out of a contract period following a:
  - ➤ contract expiry
  - ➤ contract termination

Each of these scenarios carries its own level of risk, and need to be planned, guided by a customised transition plan. Before a contract commences, a transition plan needs to be set up to cover the above scenarios in order to ensure smooth transitioning into the contractual agreement, and then transitioning out of it at an agreed time (either through termination or expiry).

When transitioning, the contract manager needs to take into account two sides of the equation: the people side (from communication to relationship management), and the process side (the mechanics).

The types of things a transition plan should consider include:

- ✓ If it is a new contractor, how stakeholders may be impacted
- ✓ Notification to stakeholders/users
- ✓ Transfer of contract material from previous contractor or from in-house setup
- ✓ How the new setup may differ from the current/previous setup
- ✓ Staff and document handover arrangements
- ✓ Knowledge management
- ✓ Operational and logistical handover
- ✓ Systems interfacing

The following diagram illustrates a number of items to take into account before and during transition.

Settling in period as the company moves from one state to another, e.g. from in-house to outsourcing.	
⬇	⬇
Processess and Systems	**People Issues**
• account transition • establishing new service agreement • first 12 months performance parameters • financial analysis • systems training and technology issues • quality assurance, benchmarking • process improvement • acceptance testing of key transition milestones • workload, project plan, critical dates, portfolio issues	Organisational issues (immediate and longer term) for human resources • employee management issues • compensation and payouts • communication protocols between parties • training programs • cultural integration • relationship building • account management • knowledge transfer
⬇	⬇
Embed new process changes as a result of cultural integration and changing business needs	

Figure 8: Transition management.

Transition management

Transition management is a term used to describe the settling in period as the company moves from one state to another, e.g. from in-house to outsourcing.

Procurement and contract managers have much to plan for and prepare. They also need to be in constant communication with the incumbent contract

Transition management

manager to appraise them of their activities and decisions, otherwise things tend to fall between the cracks. It's called the great divide, or value leakage.

Value leakage

Value leakage can occur when a company splits up its procurement function from the rest of the company as a separate function. Perceptions from both procurement people and the contract managers differ based on each of their perspectives.

Procurement people see business units as focused on:

✓ price reduction
✓ using arbitrary contract language

Contract managers see procurement people as:

✓ indifferent to cost considerations
✓ uninformed about marketplace alternatives

The key is for both parties to communicate regularly so that the 'value-for-money' equation becomes reality, taking into account all the above.

When considering value for money, it's not only about the money or the price. It's about assessing how much value one is to get from a given supplier. This is dealt with in more depth in the next chapter.

Chapter 3

CASE STUDY #2: Selecting Best Fit
"When the shoe fits..."

The business problem

The Banc Ltd had been mandated to save costs from all angles with a view to sustaining their competitive positioning in the regional marketplace.

Historically, it was one of the strongest performing banks in the country, but its price-earnings ratio had been losing ground, and its profit margins were slightly waning, so in a bid to gain momentum and retain its number one position, the bank's board had decided to save costs at all counts. The CEO had been charged to find the low hanging fruit, those areas which were costing the bank the most and which could offer the greatest cost savings through more efficient handling.

After a week-long management retreat and several heavy duty meetings at board and senior management level, it was agreed to outsource some of the banks' non-core activities, starting with the two most time consuming and labour intensive, non revenue producing areas: private mortgage lending processing and customer call centres. It was agreed that, as these areas absorbed a great deal of service time and, as much of it was transactional and repetitive, an external service provider should be sought and trained to carry out the work.

Procuring potential contractor companies

Terms and conditions for outsourcing these services were bundled up into one main contract, and after a worldwide tender process, the

Banc Ltd had narrowed down the prospective provider pool to two selected bidders. One was a local service company based in the same country, but situated off the mainland and specialising in call centres, with less experience in mortgage processing. The second was a company based offshore in India and represented by a Hong Kong agency that the Banc Ltd had had other dealings with previously. The second provider also serviced many other local and global banks with the same set of services.

Selecting best fit

The procurement team was commissioned to make the call. It had passed both prospective service companies through a rigorous selection criteria process and had evaluated each of them, which resulted in similar scores. Each presented with similar technical capabilities and processes, and seemingly similar sets of resources and experience, albeit that the offshore provider had more specific experience in the financial institution industry.

Other selection processes were required to determine the winning bidder. It was recommended that they use the best-fit scorecard (Template 2) to identify best fit on both a business and a people management level. As they had already evaluated both bidders on most of the criteria in 'business fit' (left-hand column), they assessed the bidders 'people management fit' to determine who would best qualify for the contract. They evaluated the company's track records to meet business challenges, by ringing up referees and asking specific questions about their experiences. Mixed messages came through from the reference checks. They also checked and compared each of the companies' plans for resourcing, relationship management, account management, succession and transition, and checked for evidence of previous track records in cost saving initiatives.

The evaluation process involved reviewing the written material provided, ringing through to references, and few face-to-face interview meetings to assess and verify details and questions arising. Neither company had much to say about their relationship management capabilities,and this remained an issue of concern to Banc Ltd.

The Results

The winning bidders were the service providers based in India. They were assessed as having far more industry experience, and yet the people fit was not as evident. Their references checked out reasonably well, although two referees were from another country and one other was a local competitor who had only just commenced a contract with them via the same Hong Kong based agency.

Communications started off on a shaky note, as language barriers prevented meaningful phone meetings. Many, many trips to India ensued, and many long months of frustration partly due to the lack of shared understandings between cultures and styles. Managers often wondered whether the anticipated cost savings may have been outweighed by the benefits of using a home-grown provider.

As time went on, and after a couple of hard and arduous years, the two companies established a better understanding of each other's styles and decision-making codes, especially with the help of the Hong Kong agency as a mediator, and with the help of many cultural interpretation and management workshop sessions.

CASE STUDY #2: Selecting Best Fit"When the shoe fits..."

> As the expiry date of the first term of the contract drew near, the CEO called a meeting of his heads of business units to discuss whether or not they would renew the contract.

Questions

1. Discuss the procurement decision to hire either the local or offshore service provider. Assess the virtues and disadvantages of unbundling the contract by splitting it into two separate contracts: one for call centres and the other for lending processing.

2. How could they have better measured the 'People Management Fit'?

3. How would the 'Value for Money Equation' (Chapter 3) have helped them make a decision?

4. Discuss how transition planning (figure 8) may have helped ease the new company in to the contract and working partnership.

5. Use the vendor/supplier culture map (Chapter 4) to discuss how operations could have been streamlined and/or different decisions have been made to achieve a better understanding of behavioral codes and relationship management styles.

6. Use Figure 12 (chapter 4) to map out your own contract vendor/supplier cultural mapping issues, whether they be local or offshore, noting that 'culture' can be defined as any one of generational, avocational, organisational or occupational.

Chapter 4
The Power of Outsourcing

A lot depends on the power of the relationship, and how well parties understand each other and get on together. This goes to the core of a good contract.

The matter of best-fit supplier is explored further, investigating cultural fit issues, the management of meaning and criteria evaluation. In the context of good relationship management, one needs to handle each form of contract appropriately. When dealing with companies overseas, say in an outsourcing or offshoring contract, one needs to embrace new cultures and understand even the finest of nuances.

To get a contractual relationship right, we need to zoom right in to the relationship of the parties. This chapter takes a look at the power of outsourcing, which is underpinned by the interrelationships between the people involved. It is true to say that everything we do in business has two sides to it: The people side (psychology) and the process side (mechanics).

Figure 9: Two sides of the coin.

To get a contract working and well oiled, both sides of the coin need to be balanced. **The Psychology** is about getting on with and sharing understandings with people, embracing differences and taking several parts to make a greater whole. In contract language, it means selecting the right contractual parties, and then working together on definitions of behaviour, fairness, language and other protocol. *It's about having the right techniques.*

The Process of the contract is about making sure the contract is 'engineered' appropriately so that everything is set up to work. *It's about having the right tools and processes.*

Having excellent mechanics is no guarantee for success, unless the psychology issues (the people performance and cultural integration) are ironed out from the beginning. The conundrum could be illustrated like this:

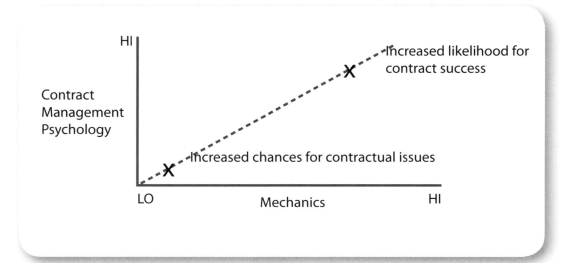

Figure 10: Contract management performance success.

I talked earlier about best-fit supplier (see Chapter 3). We now need to examine further the fit test in terms of the people side of the equation (remember, there's always a people side and a mechanical side to every business equation).

In particular, I want to focus on cultural fit issues, and the management of meaning as an important element in the evaluation of the best-fit supplier.

To gear up for new outsourcing arrangements, one needs to map the way you do business in-house and then set up a plan for stakeholder or relationship management with the other party, the outsourcing company. There is no point starting to understand what others do if you can't define your own culture on a national scale and on an individual scale.

As the world gets smaller, the more we think that others should work just as we do, and this doesn't always translate. In today's changing environment, trade contracts and outsourcing are taking on different shapes. We are almost forced into specialisations, where we seek other companies to operate parts of our own business, under our drive and direction.

With the tightening of the economy worldwide, shifts in the way we do business are happening and our fight for survival means we outsource to the best in breed, wherever they are. But with this need comes an assumption that the world is homogenising, flattening, and becoming one and the same. This is a fallacy.

Now, more than ever, we need to focus on our strengths and make our own culture and that of other trading companies visible, rather than invisible. Now, more than ever, we are seeking one major thing from outsourcing: VALUE; and within the value equation, future value is a combination of specialist skills, resources and shared understanding of the culture of those we work with.

It is true, that, from a global playing field, the world is getting flatter. According to Thomas L. Friedman, in his book *The World is Flat, a brief history of the 21st Century*, there have been 10 major 'flatteners' that have leveled the global playing field over the past two decades. The first five are externally focused, forcing us to let go of something in order to gain value. The other five are internally focused, enabling us to work smarter and faster with tools we have, whilst allowing others in the supply chain to add value to our activities.

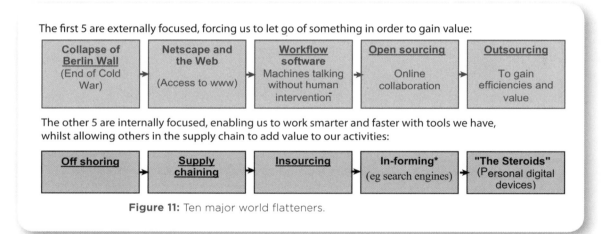

Figure 11: Ten major world flatteners.

So we have established the world is getting flatter through the use of smart tools and methodologies. But what of cultural differences? Are these smoothing over, are we all becoming part of this sameness where world business is now 'the new culture'?

Culture mapping

Culture mapping is something we should do to unravel a series of cultural realities and then state assumptions. It is a relevant tool to use whenever we partner or contract out significant pieces of work for substantial periods of time, or at any time when entering into a contract of a high risk nature.

When selecting or procuring best-fit suppliers, one must take a look at how that company/person/contractor fits one's internal company culture, and vice versa. This is even truer when such contractor or supplier is overseas, or is from a country or region other than your own. After all, significant contracts require us to spend an awful lot of time and energy with a new set of contractors/suppliers, who indeed can become one's business family.

The following tools and techniques can be applied at either a local, regional or national level, to ensure that one understands the culture of the people we are about to work with, and understands how best they fit in with our needs.

The vendor/supplier culture map

The vendor/supplier culture map is a form of relationship mapping which starts with mapping out one's own culture, as a workgroup, company, and/ or organisation. If this can be documented, it's easier then to work out how our own culture differs from others. One's own culture is, on the face of things, invisible to oneself. This exercise allows people to step out of their comfort zone, and analyse where they are in relation to style, behaviour, influence, needs, taboos and accepted norms. Once this is done, they can then map the cultures of their stakeholders, suppliers and contractors.

In this vendor/supplier culture map, people can discuss and document the kinds of culture they embrace and expect, and state assumptions about their service providers/partners as a starting point for a culture bridging discussion.

This culture mapping can drill right down to how we communicate. Once we have mapped this out, and worked on a sound communication plan, there may be a need for internal change management programs, an essential ingredient of mapping, ensuring cultural surprises don't turn into culture shock.

Depending on the type of contracting relationship one is involved with, and whether the contract is outsourced or offshored, your culture map may take up different elements. There are a number of dimensions on which culture can be mapped, and it is entirely up to you which dimension is relevant to your contractual situation.

There are four steps to the vendor/supplier culture map as follows.

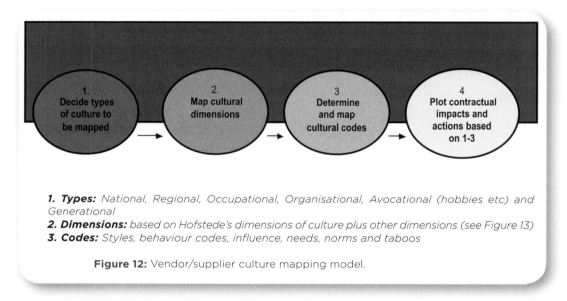

1. Types: *National, Regional, Occupational, Organisational, Avocational (hobbies etc) and Generational*
2. Dimensions: *based on Hofstede's dimensions of culture plus other dimensions (see Figure 13)*
3. Codes: *Styles, behaviour codes, influence, needs, norms and taboos*

Figure 12: Vendor/supplier culture mapping model.

A typical vendor/supplier culture map allows you to look at your own organisation and map this against that of your supplier to see where there are overlaps and differences.

Culture	Cultural Dimension	Cultural Code	Contractual Impacts	Action Required
National				
Team Composition	Team Member motivation	Individualism or Collective	Working style and expectations Need more time for personal Focus on material aspects Planning the work Decision making	Reward to include time off Inclusiveness in team incentives amount of buy in required
	Team Trust	Acknowledge abilities/ or clan mentality		Acknowledge abilities and traits Monthly face-to-face meetings
	Progress of planning	Focus on short or long term	Implications on decision making	Need to plan long term
	Decision making process & content	Legacy v material based Democratic v autocratic	Types of decisions	
Regional				
	Use of time	Task v relationship orientation	Time factor	
Organisational*	Power distance	levels of individual power	Find out who to negotiate with	
	Uncertainty Avoidance	Managing uncertainty and risk	Risk averse v flexibility	
	Individual v collective		Decision making	
	Masculine v feminine		Styles	
	Long term v short term		Time horizon	
	Hierarchical v democratic	Desire to take responsibility	Level of accountability taken	

Template 4: Example of a vendor/supplier culture map.[1]

1   *The following dimensions of organisational culture are characterized by Hofstede's culture dimension theory:

Culture Type

Template 4 takes national cultural type as an example for a vendor /supplier culture map:

✓   Power distance - the degree to which there is expected to be differences in the levels of individual power

✓   Uncertainty avoidance - the extent to which they accept uncertainty and risk. Whether people want to control the inherent uncertainty with rules, or handle the ambiguity and react flexibly deepens with one's national cultural tendencies.

✓   Individualism contrasted with collectivism - the extent to which people are expected to stand up for themselves, or alternatively act predominantly as a member of group/organisation.

✓   Masculinity versus femininity - the value placed on traditionally male or female values. Typical male values, for example, usually include competitiveness, assertiveness, ambition, and the accumulation of wealth and material possessions.

✓   Long versus short term orientation - a 'time horizon', or the importance attached to the future versus the past and present. In long term oriented cultures, thrift and perseverance are valued more; in short term oriented societies, respect for tradition and reciprocation of gifts and favors are valued more.

✓   Hierarchy - revolves around what people think about their relationships with supervisors and subordinates. Is there is a large gap or do managers expect subordinates to speak out?

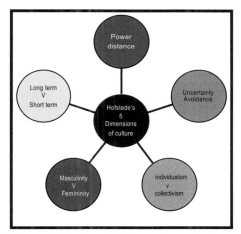

Figure 13: Hofstede's dimensions of culture.

When mapping cultures and behaviours, always map your own styles and codes first, as a group. This will make you more aware of cultural invisibility and cultural assumptions. What's happening in your own company or country may be very different to elsewhere. Never make assumptions. It's always okay to ask about these differences, but may be very rude not to, and leaving it too long may be too late in the relationship. Sort all these things up front, making every decision with a view to sustainability for the long term.

Bearing in mind that culture brings with it different dimensions, the best risk management approach is to plan and analyse all your stakeholders, those nearby and those across shores and borders, for it is this that will make the outsourcing arrangement sustainable and valuable for the future.

The use of culture mapping is to plot stakeholders' needs and styles, to know what to expect, to become transparent, and to embrace and understand the differences of your business partners.

The main idea is to work on your business relationship so that the written contracts never have to be examined. Knowing your suppliers and what drives them is more than part way to **making contracts work.**

Dimensions of culture

74

Configuring the Contract

Chapter 5
The Power of the Word

Even though this book is about far more than just the actual written contract, it would be remiss if a contract management book of this nature didn't refer to at least some of the basic terms of a contract. Focus is placed on key terms such as intellectual property, indemnity and insurance, termination and the initial recitals.

So, we worked out very early on that a contract can be a contract without even being written. There are many great law books on this topic, so this chapter is not intended to be 'Contracts 101'. However, there are a few key terms that our friend James should keep in mind when finalising his contract.

The power of the written word principle states that if something is said or agreed to but is not documented, the words have little power when push comes to shove. It goes further, to state that if agreements remain unwritten, it can lead to misunderstandings and unfounded assumptions.

There are various forms of contract and there are also endless variations of terms and conditions. The best principle is to keep everything simple and use plain English when documenting a contract, rather than legalese. This will allow for a greater shared understanding of what's expected. Indeed, once a contract is written, it's a good idea to sit down with the other party/parties and have an open workshop on how each party perceives the terms and conditions of the contract.

On the other hand, once the agreement is put into writing, or recorded in another form, one must ensure that all parties understand the industry nuances and legal language embedded in the contract.

For the purposes of this chapter, and in the name of sound risk management, let's assume there is a documented (or recorded) contract, and examine some of the main standard clauses of a contract in layman's terms. Just as most of us will need to manage a contract at some stage of our working career, most of us will need to read one and make sense of it.

The recitals

At the beginning of a contract, after the names of the parties, there is usually a section headed 'WHEREAS…'. This is technically called the recitals, and should be used to insert in very clear language the clear intent and purpose of the contract.

This is where you can use the essence of Contract Proposal (see Chapter 2, from the Plan Phase) to clarify the objectives of the contract. It should allow someone to be able to pick up the contract and say, 'Ah ha, so that's what the contract is setting out to do'. Even though it is only a paragraph or two, keep it as tight and descriptive as possible to allow for this to happen. The rest of the contract can then be read with this in mind.

Termination clause

The termination clause is an interesting and vital clause. When contracts are entered into, there is almost always the best of intentions to see the contract through, and not to stray from the agreed terms. At the commencement of negotiations for a contract, there is indeed a honeymoon period where no party can do wrong. This is the ideal time to agree on what to do in the event that something does change or go wrong, even if it is no one's fault.

This is definitely a risk management clause, and it builds flexibility into the relationship. Apart from the usual talk about negligence and non compliance, it should also discuss how and if external or environmental changes can be a cause for termination of the contract.

Contingencies for non performance of deliverables is often referred to, but be mindful that this scenario could be caused by either party. To cater for termination based on client demands outside of the agreed terms, service providers often request that the clause explicitly excludes non performance caused by client changes or requests.

Intellectual property (I.P.) clause

This is by far one of the most complex areas of the contract, particularly when it comes to service contracts and use of ideas. It is an area that should always be referred to a lawyer for advice.

Intellectual property or (IP) represents the property of your mind or intellect. It can be an invention, trade mark, original design or the practical application of a good idea. In business terms, this means your proprietary knowledge - a key component of success in business today. It is often the edge which sets successful companies apart and as world markets become increasingly competitive, protecting your IP becomes essential.

The question as to who owns the knowledge, ideas and copyright of things created out of the contract is always a matter of negotiation and contention, which needs to be agreed upon before the contract commences.

Once ownership of the IP rights is established, the owner of those rights can then license the use of them for a particular contract period. This should only entitle the licensee – the procurer or purchaser in contractual terms – to use the IP for the purpose intended under the contract, but does not entitle them to sell, exploit or commercialise the IP otherwise.

Copyright

You can protect your ideas by invoking copyright. Copyright protects the original expression of ideas, not the ideas themselves. Copyright doesn't protect you against independent creation of a similar work.

Legal actions against misuse of ideas are complicated by the fact that a number of different copyrights may exist in some works - particularly films, broadcasts and multimedia products. Suffice to say that it is always best to seek legal advice before entering into contracts regarding intellectual capital, particularly in a service environment where ideas are the basis of the service.

Digital Rights Management (DRM) is the legal term for copy or content protection for digital rights, and it is supposed to protect publishers of digital games, music and other content from casual copying of their products (other than legitimate purchase of the product for the purchaser).

It's easiest to display the variety of IP rights through industry related examples as follows:

✓ **A university**, for example, would often contract with its academics and researchers that all ideas, copyrights, designs, etc developed during their tenure at the university are owned by the university. This often presents a dilemma for researchers, for example, who, throughout the course of their work, invent or discover something new and would like to retain their rights to the findings.

✓   **In the software business**, the owner of the source code (the software language) holds the IP rights and licences them out to whoever purchases the software. So, Microsoft, who invented and created Windows, licenses out the use of their software to whoever purchases it, but always retains the ownership of the product so that they can retain the right to change, upgrade and resell their software to all and sundry.

✓   In the hardware business, IP usually belongs to the original designers of the hardware, and these rights should be covered off during the product design and engineering stage.

✓   In the music industry, 'copyright' underlies the ways people make money out of musical ideas and performance. There are so many elements to copyright, basically broken down into two areas:

➤ Works (artistic names, titles, sheet music, musical compositions, literary and dramatic)

➤ Subject matter other than works (sound recordings, live broadcasts and published editions)

In this industry, there is a clear distinction between the musical work reproduced and the recording itself. There is only one owner of the lyrics and music of 'Blue Suede Shoes', but there are hundreds of recorded versions, with the copyright of each new recording owned by the recording artist.

The general rule is that the 'author' of the song is the owner of the IP, or copyright, as it is called in that industry. The author of the music is the composer, the author of the lyrics is the lyricist, etc, and the maker of the sound recording is usually the owner of the copyright of the recording.

Copyright

✓ **In the publishing and multimedia business**, there are many levels of IP, similar to that described in the music industry above. Contracts need to deal with authorship of the ideas, contents, words, and format. The essence of these things makes up the product that, if unpublished, could diminish in value. So publishing contracts reserve the right for the publisher to publish books and digital rights, a matter to be negotiated so that value is added to the words and thoughts that make up writing a book.

✓ In service management industries, most of the value is in the creation of the ideas and thoughts required to design and innovate programs, courses, and other initiatives and projects. So it would only be fair to allow the originator and creator to retain full rights to use their ideas, etc, again and not hand over the rights to the client/purchaser of the contract forever. In reality, this is always a matter of negotiation.

Vendors of such services often wish to retain the rights to the customised portions of the program, realising that the core business of the professionals providing the service comprise the essence of the program they are providing, and such professionals need to retain the rights to use again in different shapes and forms for other clients. Often, the compromise will be to allow the vendor (purchaser/client) an exclusive right to use the programs, etc, in-house, but exclude the rights to commercialise or exploit the programs to third parties outside of their organisation.

Indemnity and insurance clauses

Again, another set of clauses to be most careful with. Many contracts ask the provider to indemnify the client against anything and everything. It is fair to ask to exclude situations which are caused by the client's own negligence or default.

This clause is often linked to insurance policies as they underwrite the provider in the event that the indemnities are called on. Insurance should cover as much as you feel is at risk. I have never come across any person or company who have suffered from over insurance, but many do from under insurance. On the other hand, always seek several quotes before entering into an insurance policy, to keep a fair market advantage and ensure that you are covered for what you need.

In a service environment, there are many types of insurance, two of the most prominent being:

✓   Professional Indemnity Insurance

Professional indemnity insurance protects professionals against claims of negligence made against them by a client. This type of insurance is available to professionals across a range of industries and covers the costs and expenses of defending a legal claim, as well as any damages payable.

Professionals are legally held to a higher degree of skill and care than ordinary people. If others suffer a loss that can be attributed to a specialist's failure to uphold professional standards, they risk being sued for a breach of professional duty. A client's loss may be material, financial or physical.

✓   Public Liability Insurance

This is a very broad term for insurance covering liability exposures for individuals and business owners. It generally includes all exposures for property damage and bodily injury, except exposures that relate to ownership of airplanes and automobiles, and to employees.

Variation clauses

Many variation clauses state that the contract cannot be varied unless by agreement between all parties in writing. Although this is a standard clause, it would be wise to set up flexibility mechanisms by referring to a schedule of possible variations with criteria for such variations, and triggers for their acceptance or rejection. More about this in Chapter 9.

This chapter presents the third stage of the contract management lifecycle – manage. It considers performance management in both lead indicator and lag indicator terms, setting out a sound contract management measurement model for strategic and operational issues.

The concept of contract risk management underpins this chapter, and is woven into the fabric of the contract framework.

Remember principle two of the contract management framework: measurability. You can't manage what you can't measure. So setting up performance standards which are measurable – quantitatively and qualitatively – is really the only way you can monitor progress and results. This may sound obvious, but too many contracts are open-ended when it comes to measurability, leaving all parties out in the cold when things go awry.

Let's get back to James' case. Remember he was lumped with trying to finalise a contract that he hadn't negotiated, that he wasn't familiar with and that he wasn't comfortable with finalising.

He had gotten over the governance side of making sure that the people (who his boss lunched with regularly) were actually the most worthy of doing the job. He did this by working through the best-fit scorecard (figure 7, Chapter 3). He also attempted a pitted version of the vendor/supplier culture map (see Chapter 4) in order to prove that either they were or weren't the right people for the job. Good on him, because if either of these tools proved there was a high risk in hiring them, he had this down for the record, and, if he could summon up the gumption, he could present this to his boss.

Now he felt he had come to a milestone. This was the real test of how he could manage the end bit of the 'procure' phase. It was about setting up targets and performance indicators that could, during the management stage, muster the test of the four 'R's', as in:

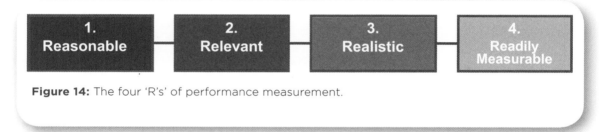

Figure 14: The four 'R's' of performance measurement.

James will see that, with good solid planning throughout the 'Plan' and 'Procure' stages, performance of the supplier becomes more relevant and realistic, rather than a penalty driven exercise.

Stage Three ("Manage")

Let's revert back to the structure of the contract management lifecycle, just to make sure that James is on track. Based on the contract management framework, we are now up to the third stage of the lifecycle of the contract management methodology, 'Manage', as shown in Figure 3c.

This 'Manage' stage is what most other people call 'contract management'. However, we now know that contract management spans across the planning and procurement of the goods/services well before the contract is finalised or signed.

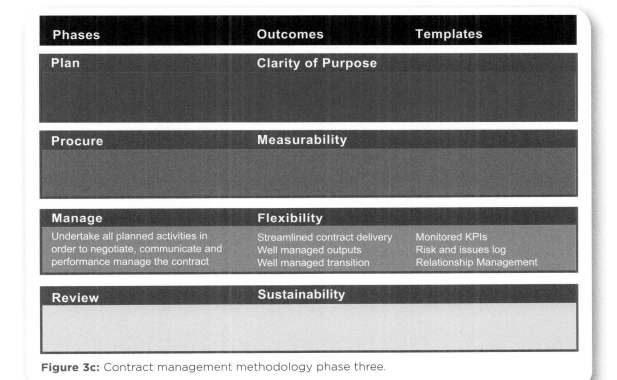

Phases	Outcomes	Templates
Plan	**Clarity of Purpose**	
Procure	**Measurability**	
Manage Undertake all planned activities in order to negotiate, communicate and performance manage the contract	**Flexibility** Streamlined contract delivery Well managed outputs Well managed transition	Monitored KPIs Risk and issues log Relationship Management
Review	**Sustainability**	

Figure 3c: Contract management methodology phase three.

This third stage in the contract management Lifecycle, 'Manage', is where flexibility is needed in action, requiring the art of negotiation to be managed within agreed terms and conditions. There are several parts to this stage, and we will examine each part separately:

- ✓ Performance measurement (KPI's)
- ✓ Sound risk management
- ✓ Relationship management (covered in Chapter 7)

Performance measurement (KPIs)

It's important to focus on why you are measuring as well as what and how you measure.

Bear in mind that there are eight categories of management reasons as to why performance is measured in contracts, including:

→ Evaluate
→ Control
→ Budget
→ Motivate
→ Promote
→ Celebrate
→ Learn
→ Improve

When you formulate the actual indicators or measurement parameters, it's important to focus on these reasons so that the measurement indicators are aligned to the outcomes you desire from the contract. For example, if the

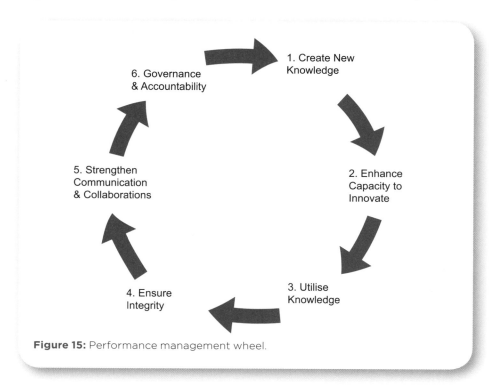

Figure 15: Performance management wheel.

ultimate outcome of the contract is to have a more efficient system in place, as in James' case, then setting up a measurement tool which will require intense reporting and constant micro-management does not lead itself to efficiency overall.

So when setting up the measuring indicators, or Key Performance Indicators (KPIs) as they are called, keep in mind the ultimate outcome.

When you are thinking about measurement strategically, you can use the Performance Measurement Wheel (see figure 15), then under each of the categories appearing, list what is most important in that category to measure from a practical sense. This orders our mind and also aligns whatever we are measuring with what we are setting out to achieve (outcomes).

In terms of envisaged change from new contracts (especially service-based contracts), performance can be measured under the headings set out in Figure 15, starting with:

1. The creation of new knowledge (as knowledge is power) that enables
2. Capacity to innovate, and then
3. Utilise the new knowledge.

All these new ideas and innovations need to be grounded by:

4. Integrity (integrity of data, of people and of systems).

Then the measurement wheel turns to:

5. Communicating about/with the newly gained knowledge and innovation, acting on, and collaborating with it.

The entire measurement wheel is underpinned by:

6. The governance and accountability of service or product delivery and outcomes.

The beauty of this wheel is that most other measurement frameworks start with number 6: governance and accountability. Our wheel has five strong spokes in it to step through before we even reach the critical part of accountability and governance.

A good contract manager should use some, or all, of these 'headings' when setting up measurement parameters for their contract. For example, starting with parameter 1: 'creating new knowledge', you need to place a measurement to this that makes sense in your context. If the contract is for the outsourcing of a call centre, creating new knowledge is very relevant: it could mean a thing as simple as each call centre operator asking a separate set of questions from the customer to decipher where most of the queries come from, by asking their postcode and then compiling this into a monthly report. It could be as deep as finding out whether they have used other substitute products or services previously and why they chose this one as a result, which could be compiled into a competitor analysis report, adding more value to each customer profile.

What you measure: lag vs lead indicators

There are a number of different things to measure in a contract, depending on the nature of the contract. Measurables should consist equally of lag indicators and lead indicators.

Lag indicators are historical results that occurred in the past, e.g. was the customer satisfied last month? Lead indicators follow patterns of usage, showing patterns of satisfaction over a 12-month period, with, say, customer incidents, which become convertible into forecastable trends, or indicators, for the coming 12 months. A good set of performance measures in a contract should have an equal spread of both lag and lead indicators.

Lead indicators measure:	Lag Indicators enable:
• Process	• Measurement of goal achievement
• Patterns of usage	• Evaluation of success
• Ongoing feedback alerting managers to changes/variations	• Assessment of benefits over period of time
eg. Client feedback Incidents	eg. Client satisfaction

Figure 16: Lead and lag performance indicators.

When measured and monitored effectively, lead indicators provide data to enable effective intervention to address or reverse a negative trend.

Monitoring performance

James needs to have a regime in place in order to monitor performance. Given that the four Rs (see figure 14, page 86) were taken into account when setting up the measurements, one would expect them to be meaningful and realistic. The main steps that a contract manager should take when monitoring performance are to:

✓ Review contract performance for progress and compliance;

✓ Communicate with contractors to maximise performance in line with strategic intent;

✓ Set up a payment plan in line with contract provisions and applicable law for standards; and

✓ Maintain all records for reporting and also for future verification.

This can be a lot of work and hence our four Rs system, which make the measurement meaningful. If the contract has a complex set of performance measures, then it would be worth hiring someone in-house to monitor and report on contractor performance, rather then relying on reports from the contractor, as these could be biased or skewed. It will also allow the contractor to concentrate on performance rather than spend too much of their time reporting. The best scenario is for both sides to have their own performance monitors who could liaise regularly to ensure there is congruence in performance and delivery.

There are so many ways one can measure and report on performance. The main thing is that it is done in a way that works. It's important that the Key Performance indicators (KPIs) are set up in a way that that makes it possible to measure them, and that they are indeed performance-driven,

Task Driven	Performance driven
Buyer specifies work process	Contractor specifies specific work process
It's a 'what's in it for me' relationship	It's a mutual consequences relationship
Contractor selection is price driven	Contractor selection is capability driven
No interim consequences for poor work	Incentives/deductions for performance
Contractor does not "bid spec"	Contractor bids outcomes and results
Focus on cost reduction	Focus on company competitive advantage
Use controls and systems as directed	Use controls and systems constantly
Do what is needed to do job	Find and implement best practice
Buyer assumes performance risks	Contractor assumes performance risks
Greater co-employment risks	Little co-employment risks
Contractor accountable for buyers system	Contractor accoutnable for own system
Success based on the worker	Success based on the system
Problem fixing management strategy	Process improvement management strategy
Buyer manager the job	Contractor manages the job
Responsiveness + problem fixing = success	Problem prevention + results = success
Goals are focused on short term savings	Golas are focused on long term value
	Contractor selection is price driven

Figure 17: Task-driven vs performance-driven contracts.

rather than task-driven. Otherwise, you may find yourself in a position of micromanaging, which is usually not what is intended when one contracts out. Let me illustrate this as follows:

Using the points in figure 17, if you give your contract a score out of 16, with one point for each performance driver, and subtracting one point for each task driver, you can reflect on how your KPIs are set out, and why it would be more strategic to measure performance rather than tasks. Advantages of performance-driven contracts include offering incentives for achieving goals. ie allowing the contractor flexibility to get a job done.

Example 1
- ✓ In a task-driven approach the buyer would specify the task and frequency of the work.
- ✓ In a performance-driven approach, the contractor specifies the process.

Example 2
- ✓ In a task-driven approach, the focus is on reducing costs.
- ✓ In a performance-driven approach, the goal is on value and gaining competitive advantages.

Performance standards and indicators

A performance standard is what we measure, and a performance indicator is how we measure it. A very simple operational example is as follows:

KPIs are the critical success measures which help an organisation define and measure its progress toward set organisational goals and operational indicators. Operational indicators measures relate to the day-to-day operational facilities management activities.

Roles	Tasks	Performance Standards	Performance Indicators (KPIs)
Office management	Answering phones	Number of rings	Within 3 rings
	Providing customer service	Follow up hours/days	Within 24 hours
	Entering data	Number of words/minute	60 words/minute
	Ordering materials	Money spent on consumables	Not exceeding % of budget

Figure 18: Difference between performance standards and performance indicators (KPIs).

The challenge is making the choice of indicators and measures valid, reliable and efficient to administer. So, when setting up your performance indicator framework, be strategic:

✓   Link performance indicators and measures to:
➤ Business goals
➤ Critical success factors
➤ Stakeholder needs and expectations

✓   Incorporate both lead and lag indicators

Here are some questions to seek resolution on when setting up your KPI framework. Once you have outlined the key areas of measurement (use the Performance Measurement Wheel, figure 15), you can ask the following questions to decipher performance monitoring:

1.   **Measure** – what is the title of the measure

2.   **Purpose** – what is the aim of the measure

3.   **Target** – what level of performance is desirable/achievable?

4.   **Formula** – what formula is required to explain which data?

5.   **Frequency** – how often should the measure by made/reported?

6.   **Who** – who is responsible for measuring/reporting?

7.   **Source** – where will the data to make this measure come from?

8.   **Action plan** – what actions will the contractor take to ensure that performance along this dimension improves?

Likely areas of measurability:

Quality
- ✓   Customer satisfaction
- ✓   Effective service delivery

Continuous improvement
- ✓   Value for money
- ✓   Asset management

Risk

- ➤   Environmental management
- ➤   Risk management

Performance standards and indicators

KPI scorecard

When monitoring performance, there are a variety of measures you can use to score KPIs, as follows:

Objective method of scoring for each performance measure:

5   Catastrophic -- absence causes failure to entire systems

4   Critical -- absence causes failure to major components

3   Major -- absence causes failure to systems component

2   Intermediate -- major impact to daily process/procedures

1   Minor -- minor impact to daily process/procedures

Scoring when objective method of scoring is not possible:

5   Excellent – innovation and re-engineering qualities achieved (reward/bonus kicks in)

4   Very good – has met target requirements/expectations

3   Good – has met requirements but improvements required

2   Average – has partially met requirements

1   Poor (has not met any requirements,100% penalty applies)

Template 5: KPI Scorecard

Risk/reward models

Risk and reward sharing is a feature of partnering or alliance contracts. This model is based on achieving certain defined performance metrics resulting from the services provided. The risk/reward framework for a contract provides financial incentives/disincentives based on delivery of contract outcomes that would represent value for money (especially in comparison to more traditional principal/contractor arrangements).

The purpose of a risk/reward model is to ensure there is a mutual sharing of 'pain and gain', related to contract outcomes. There are six attributes for the setting up of a risk/reward set of performance measures. It must:

1. Be simple and easy to understand
2. Drive alliance/partnering behaviour in an appropriate way (openness and transparency)
3. Be SMART (Simple, Measurable, Applicable, Relevant and Timely)
4. Guide the measurement process
5. Contribute to achieving broader client goals and business objectives, making it beneficial to all parties, and
6. Be adjustable if major changes occur

A good way to set this up for each measurable is to place an actual measure, an original target and a score such as this service-related example:

Performance Wheel Spoke	Indicator	Measure	Comment	Original Target	Possible Score	Score
Eg strengthened communication and collaboration	Eg Customer Satisfaction	Eg Feedback survey to gain perspective of service delivery & relationship building	Eg Competed	>95%	8	
				90%-95%	6	
				85%-90%	4	
				80%-85%	2	
					0	

Template 6: Risk/reward rating table.

*The Annual 'at risk' Fee distribution schedule is based on total score of original targets met. So, for example, if the total score column adds up to :

90-100 points: then 100% of the 'at Risk Fee' would be payable

80-89 points: then 85% of the 'at Risk Fee' would be payable

75-79 points: then 75% of the 'at Risk Fee' would be payable

71-74 points: then 50% of the 'at risk Fee' would be payable

<70%:   then 0% of the 'at Risk Fee' would be payable

Sound Risk Management

There are volumes written on models for risk management in contracts. From a contract point of view, however, it all depends on the size of the contract and the level of complexity as to how one manages risk.

Risk, in this context, is defined as contractual risk, in terms of what could go wrong, i.e.:

✓   What if the provider goes bankrupt or is negligent or closes shop?

✓   What if the quality indicators are not met?

✓   What if the vendor changes their mind?

✓   What if the budget is blown?

✓   What if you get sued/need to sue?

These are all legitimate contractual risks that need to be thought through prior to the contract being signed, so everyone knows the level playing field.

Risk logging

The underlying parameter for sound risk management is that someone, somewhere in your organisation has to be accountable for the risk and make sure it is monitored. If not, a larger risk awaits, that of planning but not managing the plan. A simple risk management 'living' document can be set up to:

✓   provide a mechanism to regularly and openly discuss risks/ issues that may effect the deliverables of the contract;

✓   have a shared understanding about what they are and strategies to reduce them;

✓   outline who is responsible for what action to manage the risk/ issue and by when.

(*refer to the risk rating table to assist you in determining risk rating)

Description of risk	Risk Rating* (high, medium, low)	Strategy to manage risks/issues	Accountable person	By When

Template 7a: Risk log

A typical risk log could contain a risk rating table. This table will help you manage the risk by determining whether the risk rating is low, medium or high.

Risk Rating Table

Likelihood/Probability				
High	Medium Risk	High Risk	**High risk**	
Medium	**Low risk**	**Medium risk**	High risk	
Low	Low risk	Low risk	Medium Risk	
	Low	Medium	High	

Consequences/Impact

Template 7b: Risk rating table.

LIKELIHOOD/ PROBABILITY				
High	Medium Risk	High Risk	High Risk
Medium	Low Risk	Medium Risk	High Risk
High	Low Risk	Low Risk	Medium Risk
	Low	Medium	High
Impact/consequences			

Template 7c: Risk rating

We have looked at two of the three critical pillars of the 'manage' stage of the contract management lifecycle: performance management and risk management. Although these are critical pillars, the third stage merits its own chapter…relationship management.

CASE STUDY #3 - Measurability
"You can't manage what you you can't measure"

The Business Problem

Global Engineering Services (GES) were one of the larger global business and technology service companies, servicing and warehousing the electronic transaction exchanges of many large manufacturing entities and credit card companies. Their premises comprised large data warehouses that computed and interchanged information so that products such as critical medical equipment and services such as retail credit card transactions took place quickly, efficiently and without error. Suffice to say that their services were 'mission critical'. One small technical error could cost GES and their stakeholder's penalties in the millions of dollars.

At a time when clients were becoming more demanding and electrical equipment becoming more sophisticated and hi-tech, their urgent investment in new data equipment to manage their client services became an imperative. The investment required was significant and, in order to find the capital, they decided to use their internal resources to work strategically on business development and client revenue improvement.

In a blitz to relieve their internal people of the transactional non-core services, they decided to carve up some of the day-to-day low-value activities and out task them to specialist technical companies. This, they believed, would free management up to focus on relationship management to improve value add to existing customers, and boost business development activities with a view to increasing revenue-making opportunities.

The first cab off the rank was the services that their middle management spent most of their day managing -- the facility management of their data warehouses. This involved technical aspects of mechanical and electrical testing, quality checking, security, repair and maintenance, and cleaning the hardware that constituted their jewels in the crown — the machines that carried and housed their data repositories.

The performance management indicators

In addition to becoming more effective as a company, a major challenge facing GES was the reduction of energy consumption in their buildings which were rated as 5 stars from a green building perspective. They had a business imperative to reduce energy during the operational phases of their facilities life in order to reduce carbon emissions. Building audits carried out some 10 years prior on a select few buildings they operated in (some of which they had since vacated) showed that 30-40% of their total carbon emissions were attributable to their facilities, and so facility management had a significant role to play.

They set up a strict performance management regime, focusing on cost savings and carbon emission reductions. The only problem was that they had very little current data against which to compare results. They would be monitoring performance based on guesstimates of current status rather than actual figures.

After the arduous procurement process, they selected a hybrid group of companies to manage their facilities, with the head contract held by a property management company who didn't have a background in the technicalities of facility management, but who did know how to manage people. Together they set up a rigid regime of performance management indicators, partly comprising lag indicators such as cost savings achieved, but also adding in a few lead indicators, such as customer feedback incidents measured through their call centre.

Their contract included a general throw away requirement for value add and innovative practices, but over the years the service providers confessed there was no room/time for the 'luxury' of extra innovation because they were focused on the day-to-day transactional activities to be logged and measured as part of their performance management indicator regime.

Results

After a period of three years, GES were not happy. Their facility management service providers were not really adding value. They couldn't see any real cost savings as promised, the service providers hadn't demonstrated much innovation, and they felt they had gone backwards in many ways. One example was the green council's report that downgraded their buildings and facility by one star, and they blamed their service provider for not being on top of this.

They didn't know whether to terminate the contract, or renew based on a set of new or revised performance indicators, or break it down into two contracts, one for property management and the other for facility management. They didn't want to revert to the option of managing a myriad of subcontractors themselves, because although cost savings had not been established they didn't have the in-house resources anymore to do this. They had spent years investing in a partnering relationship, and they got on very well with the contractors, many of whom were based full-time at GES offices and were almost like part of the company.

Questions

1. What would you advise? Is it better to keep the service provider as 'the devil they know' with a revised set of performance indicators, using their current data for the past three years as a starting benchmark, or should they re-tender the services?

2. Using the performance management wheel (figure 15) set out a series of performance indicators in the form of measurable and monitorable strategic and operational metrics that would allow GES to operationalise knowledge management and innovation.

3. Focusing on the elements set out in figure 17, discuss how a service provider can be better driven using performance drivers rather than task-driven types of contracts.

Relationships & Negotiation

Chapter 7
The Power of Contract Relationship Management

This is where the art of contract management takes shape and in order to best manage a contract a good contract manager should be armed with a good toolkit

The toolkit in this chapter includes setting out a relationship management plan, reviewing stakeholder needs and who is responsible for each stakeholder. It allows each party to work out negotiation tactics before they are needed, sometimes in a very transparent fashion. That's the value of relationship management, it allows for equivalence as far as is possible, so that contract management doesn't set up 'sides', but rather a partnering arrangement.

Relationship management (*the art of contract management*)

It's always better to put the contract away in the drawer and work things out with your business partner. Using the flexibility mechanisms that have been discussed in earlier chapters can help you ensure there is some due process in the arrangement. However, without sound relationship management between you and your vendor/supplier/partner/alliance, nothing will help, and issues and challenges are likely to arise.

The golden rule of relationship management is that we like those who are like ourselves. So in James' case (see Chapter 1), because his boss liked the people, he intimated to James to make the contract with them work. That's life in the world of business. Clearly it's not due process, it doesn't follow all the rules of the contract management framework, but it happens.

The secret of relationship management is to understand what behaviours you need to adopt to get along with people who do not share your core emotional drives, and to have the flexibility to modify your own behaviour. We discussed this earlier in our culture mapping exercise (see Chapter 4).

Setting up a good relationship is about everything we have talked about so far: understanding the 'other side' and indeed acting as if there are no sides. This shared understanding incorporates understanding the blend of business and other cultures, as well as having a shared set of ground rules to know how to behave, and who and what to expend energy on (see Chapter 6 for examples of performance measurement). Most of all, the terms and conditions of the contract need to represent the agreement and be understood by all parties (see Chapter 3 re aligning understandings regarding the heads of agreement).

Once all this is in place, it is time to focus on the people. Remember the two sides of the coin (figure 9, chapter 4). It's the people that matter most of all. If the people have a shared understanding, know where they stand, and basically know the 'rules of engagement', or how to 'play the game', then things seem to fall into place.

Bearing in mind that contract management is largely a people process, each of the parties should:

- ✓ write down what it thinks the contract says and compare understandings before signing
- ✓ redesign service delivery to incorporate inter-organisational exchanges, and
- ✓ work together to manage change, incorporating flexibility into the contract for maximum mutual benefit

How do you ensure that this can happen? One tool I recommend and use is a Relationship Management Plan. There are many aspects to relationship management, but it's best to start planning during the 'honeymoon period' whilst a relationship is at its best, but newest stage.

The relationship management plan

Bear in mind that the relationship management plan not only includes different entities of various parties, it also involves the stakeholders – those people who are impacted by the contract outcomes, but who may not be direct parties to the contract. A contract can involve quite a web of relationships, which is why it's good to map it out.

This relationship planning template allows each contract manager and his/her team to analyse the key parties of the contract, and those impacted otherwise, and see where the 'power base' lies. This is important so that each contract manager can decide how to allocate their scarce resources of time and people, and on whom to expend their energies, and to whom to allocate/delegate accountability in terms of the relationship.

Key things to focus on here are the party/stakeholder needs, their level of influence and channels of communication, thus:

Key parties	Stakeholder prioritised needs	Accountabilities & time frames	Level of influence for negotiated variations	Risks and mitigation strategies	Channels & frequency of comms.
Party 1			(see stakeholder power planning below)		
Party 2					
Party 3					
Party 4					
Stakeholder 1					
Stakeholder 2					

Template 8: Relationship mapping

In order to decipher where the power lies in the hierarchy of stakeholders, and therefore how much energy to expend on each stakeholder at any point in time, you can also plot the power base and influence of the stakeholders using this simple stakeholder analysis plan:

Stakeholder Name	Level of power and influence of stakeholder			Impact of change on stakeholder			Stakeholder attitude towards change			Level of cooperation required from stakeholder		
	High	Med	Low	High	Med	Low	Enthusiastic	Indifferent	Resistant	Necessary	Desired	Unnecessary

Template 9a: Stakeholder power mapping

Once you have plotted the power base and influence of the stakeholders using the stakeholder analysis plan you can then plot change impacts on each stakeholder against stakeholder attitudes, to gauge who could be the 'blockers' or 'gatekeepers', and who could be the 'supporters'.

Impact of the contract and its change on the stakeholders		Blockers or gatekeeps		Supporters
	High			
	Medium			
	Low			
		Resistant	**Indifferent**	**Enthusiastic**

Template 9b: Stakeholder positioning map

Try this out next time you start a new contractual relationship, especially if you have a contract team working with/for you. Bear in mind that the stakeholder power planning should be an internal document only, whilst most of the relationship mapping (except the influencing column) should be discussed with your business parties/suppliers.

Making relationships work, with the main outcome(s) in mind, lies at the heart of the power of *Making Contracts Work.*

The relationship management plan

Chapter 8
The Power of Negotiation

This chapter explores the process of contract negotiation, from beginning to end. It talks about the do's and don't's of contract negotiation, and more so about what works and what doesn't, using a case example.

The question of how one can negotiate within the letter of the law and within the wording of a contract is examined.

Don't view negotiation as an activity that ends with the signing of the contract. Negotiation is a supplier relationship management competency. A good contract manager should be in a continual state of negotiation in order to:

Reasons for continual negotiation

✓ maximise relationships within changing environments;
✓ build organisation-wide capabilities;
✓ ensure coordination amongst those interacting with suppliers, &
✓ strengthen relationships between procurement and business units.

When negotiation is not treated as an ongoing state, certain things suffer:

What could go wrong?

✓ Quality and/or service levels do not meet expectations
✓ Contract pricing could be undermined by poorly-managed scope or volume changes
✓ Expected innovation by suppliers that does not materialise
✓ Contract compliance monitoring costs could be higher than expected, and
✓ Relationships might not adapt to technology changes or shifts in market demand

Negotiation strategies

After a supplier is selected, I would recommend developing a contract negotiation strategy, starting with your objectives. Bear in mind, however, that as a buyer of goods and services, an inappropriate negotiation objective is to bleed every last cent out of the supplier for the lowest price. Remember, you want to 'partner' with your supplier so that both of you will meet your corporate goals and objectives by signing the contract.

Successful contract negotiation means to look for positives that benefit all parties and at the same time achieve a fair and equitable deal. A signed contract that benefits all parties will provide a firm foundation to build a long lasting relationship. The word 'negotiation in languages other than English, (such as Chinese) actually comprises of two words: 'give' and 'take'. Remember that.

This contract negotiation strategy form can be completed to clarify current and future issues:

STEPS	Strategic questions to clarify
1. Clarify objectives	• Clarify the terms and conditions. • What exactly is being provided, and for what purpose? • Clarify compensation, including total cost, other costs, payment schedule and financing terms. • Clarify timelines of effective dates, completion/termination dates, and renewal dates. • Classify potential risks and liabilities. • Set reasonable expectations for this relationship now and into the future.
2. List your priorities, then rank them in order of importance	• Make sure that what is most important to you is discussed and agreed upon before you move to less important items. • Refer to the least important items if you have to give up something to get your top item. • Review your priorities often during the contract negotiations planning process. Ask the hard question for each priority: 'Is this really a priority for our company, or is it a "nice to have"?'
3. Know your bottom line	• At what point will you walk away? • Is there a cost or hourly fee that your company cannot exceed? • Which of the top priorities truly non-negotiable ie a deal breaker? • List the non-negotiables with their rationale so as not to forget them.
4. Work out your BATNA[1] (Best Alternative To a Negotiated Agreement)	• Work out your BATNA (what your other alternatives to a negotiated agreement would be) and keep it in reserve as a fall-back during the negotiation. • A BATNA gives far greater flexibility and allows much more room for innovation than a predetermined bottom line.
5. Define time constraints & benchmarks	Set your expectations for performance measurement standards. • What penalty/incentives will you set/instill? • What is the potential for something to go wrong?
6. Assess potential liabilities and risks	• What if unforeseen costs are encountered? • Who will be responsible if compliance issues or government regulations are violated? • Whose insurance will cover contract workers?

1 coined by Roger Fisher and William Ury of the Harvard Business School, in their series of books on Principled Negotiation

Negotiation strategies

STEPS	Strategic questions to clarify
7. Confidentiality, dispute resolution, changes	• What do you consider to be 'confidential' information? • Who assumes liability if confidentiality is breached?
8. Complete the above steps for the 'other party' (walk in their shoes)	Now that you have completed the contract negotiations planning process for your business, repeat the same process for the other side, asking yourself from their perspective: • What area do you think is most important for them? • What risks or liabilities will they want you to assume? This is how great partnerships between client and suppliers can be developed.
9. Preparation	Before the actual contract negotiations begin, review and confirm: • If you need legal representation - If you feel the least bit uncomfortable reviewing contract 'legalese', seek legal expertise. • Location of negotiations - Agree upon where the negotiation session(s) will take place. If you think you have the upper-hand by negotiating at your offices, then propose up front that they should travel to them. If the distance is too far to travel cost effectively, set up a teleconference to accomplish the negotiation session. Make sure it is a video conference because body language speaks louder than words (see Chapter 3 on cultural mapping). • Authority to negotiate - It would be a waste of time to hear at the end of a long negotiation session 'Well, let me get back to you after I hear what my boss has to say about this.'

Template 10: Contract strategy negotiation form

Tips and techniques in contract negotiation

When setting up your negotiation keep in mind the following tips and techniques:

1. Research who/what you are dealing with.

Research your supplier/buyer/marketplace /environmental influences, don't just consider WIFM ('what is in it for me'). The larger the contract, the more time you should spend on this (See Chapter 7 for relationship management tools, figures 16-18).

2. Don't be fenced in.
Don't assume that only a limited set of conditions or resources can be negotiated. Finding creative and innovative alternatives that can benefit both parties will result in a better negotiated contract. Do not propose absurd or offensive options that will destroy your credibility and integrity.

3. Work out your BATNA (Best Alternative To a Negotiated Agreement)
A common practice used by procurement managers in the business world is to use their BATNA to leverage a better deal from their supplier, by obtaining quotes from other like companies. BATNA is the course of action a party takes if the current negotiations fail and an agreement cannot be reached. BATNA is the key focus and the driving force behind a successful negotiator. Make sure, though, that deals are properly valued, taking into account relationship value, time, value for money and the likelihood that the other party will be true to the agreement. These other considerations are often difficult to value, being often based on uncertain or qualitative factors, rather than more quantifiable measures.

4. Don't be too aggressive

Sensitivity to your colleagues will do justitce to the contract outcomes. Aggressiveness will usually raise alarm bells and defense mechanisms, making negotiations fruitless.

5. Don't just focus on price

See the earlier section on value for money (Chapter 3). Nobody wants to pay too much for their goods and services, but there is a lot more on the table than just money. So that all parties feel like they haven't been too compromised, look for alternatives that are high on your priority list and low on the other parties' priority list.

6. Take time to consider the offer

No matter how low the opening price is, see if there are other things you can ask for. If you jump too quickly at the first offer, the other party will feel like they made a mistake. The objective is to let everyone leave the negotiation table feeling like they haven't been 'sold' to or dealt the short straw.

7. Don't claim victory

When you do end up striking a fantastic deal in your favour, allow the others to save face, a particularly important concept in Asian cultures. If the other party really feels shafted, they could seek loop-holes in the contract to regain some ground back. Also, this is supposed to be a partnering relationship, rather than a 'them against us' approach.

8. Clarify 'legalese' and technical terms.

Clearly define every area of the contract, especially legal or technical terms, so that everyone is on the same page. Don't assume people know or that you share common understandings. Go to the extent of listing your assumptions separately and then compare notes.

9. Check for inconsistencies within the contract

Iron out inconsistencies, and, if necessary, have a lawyer or other independent person review the contract in order to uncover any.

10. Don't repeat clauses in different ways.

Too much clarification through repeating the same thing twice in different sections of the contract will not necessarily reinforce their value. In most instances lawyers and the courts will come up with a reason to differentiate and justify both areas; sometimes with an interpretation that neither party anticipated.

Tips and techniques in contract negotiation

CASE STYUDY #4: Designing flexibility
"Bend it, don't break it"

The Business Problem

Supply Chain Co was a newly merged company poised to dominate the local transport industry in the area of metropolitan passenger transport. Supply Chain Co was formed via a series of acquisitions of several smaller companies, including part of a government business enterprise that owned rail assets and infrastructure. Although the structure of Supply Chain Co was corporate, it had rehired many of the older employees from the government business enterprise, and with them came legacy systems, politics and processes they weren't too quick to relinquish.

The CEO of Supply Chain Co was determined to make Supply Chain Co a nifty, smart company with a competitive edge. In every dealing and with each business plan, she insisted that flexibility be built into the programs. Their new philosophy was 'bend it, don't break it'.

In building in flexibility mechanisms, an opportunity arose to look at some new contracts being put into place, with the support of the Transport Workers Union, to repair and restore rail lines. This was a highly political set of contracts because the State Government had announced it was investing in railways in the previous election and hadn't yet done so. Even though most of the funding for the repairs and maintenance would come from Supply Chain Co, the State Government were pushing for the contracts to be signed by a set date, regardless of cost concerns.

Flexibility Mechanisms

Agility remained an imperative. Despite all odds, the CEO and her executive team trawled through every contract ensuring flexibility was built in to protect Supply Chain Co from cost overruns and quality issues. It drove the unions wild, and although time was running out to get the contracts signed, the CEO forged ahead. Her main two directives were to include room for negotiation with every commercial term, and for her contract managers to complete and deliver a comprehensive set of stakeholder management plans. The lawyers were also tearing their hair out trying to make the clauses bendable but not breakable.

Time had now run out. Negotiation and stakeholder management became imperatives that were not included in some of the contracts due to lack of time, interest or understanding. 'These new fangled management terms are just slowing us down. The transport industry knows it customers, and stakeholder management is a touchy feely subject,' stated one disgruntled employee in his exit interview.

Results

The State Government had reached its tether. Its State Opposition was claiming that the government never keeps its promises, and with the next election looming they had to act fast. The contracts weren't signed, so they used safety concerns as a reason and fired the CEO in her tracks.

CASE STYUDY #4: Designing flexibility"Bend it, don't break it"

Using political clout, it influenced the hiring of a seasoned political government retiree who finalised and signed off the contracts within a week and the matter was put to bed. That is, until the contractors revved up the unions and asked for more money, more time and better facilities. The company was in a state of havoc. It almost went under, but managed to pull through this hairy period and somehow make it all look good. The State government winged it into the next election.

Questions

1. How could the CEO have saved the situation without losing her role? Would a public declaration of her previous successful corporate experience in stakeholder management and negotiation have helped, or should she have just rolled over and let it be?

2. How would using the BATNA technique (see Template 9) have helped solve the situation and implemented a quick technique for flexibility? Take an example of a typical clause you have come across that you may feel is too rigid, and set your BATNA.

3. Using the contract negotiation strategy (Template 9) as a basis for discussion, work out ways the CEO could have negotiated her way through the contracts, incorporating negotiable clauses throughout the rail contracts to ensure flexibility for the future.

4. Using the template for stakeholder management in templates 7, 9a and 9b, plot a map of how this could have been better handled. Who were the blockers and who were the supporters? Would the Union have been a key stakeholder to the situation/contracts? Take a look at a completed example below and discuss whether you agree or disagree.

An example of how Supply Chain Co could have mapped their stakeholders
is as follows:

Stake-holder Name	Level of power and influence of stakeholder			Impact of change on stakeholder			Stakeholder attitude towards change			Level of cooperation required from stakeholder		
Eg.	High	Med	Low	High	Med	Low	Enthusiastic	Indifferent	Resistant	Necessary	Desired	Unneces-sary
Union	X			X					X	X		
Rail contractor #1		X		X				X		X		
State govt rep	X				X			X			X	

IMPACT OF CONTRACT	High	X UNIONS (Blockers or Gatekeepers)	X Rail contractors	Supporters
	Medium	(X State Government Opposition)	X State Government	
	Low			
		Resistant	Indifferent	Enthusiastic

Attitude towards the change

Template 9b: Example using stakeholder positioning map

Contract Review and Lessons Learned

Review and variations are essential parts of the contract framework, and although it is deemed as stage four it indeed is relevant at various transition points in the contract management framework. Risk can escalate at any point where transition occurs as a result of change from external forces (such as legislative changes), internal forces (such as management or process changes) or change of suppliers or needs, risks can escalate.

This part of the contract framework deals with how to manage the biggest risk of all: managing transitions and change, which could lead to reviews, renewals or terminations. The message in this chapter is setting your contract up for sustainability, and offers various examples as a clue to how this could be done in a variety of settings.

James' boss, Mr Teflon, arrives back from overseas. He's raring to go, and bursts open the door of James' office, asking the state of the ITD contract and whether all went well. James is taken aback, as he rarely has the opportunity to interact with his boss, who is either away or busy. Now he feels he's been caught out, even though he's done what his boss wanted. He definitely feels, though, he can't be held accountable for the outcomes of the contract.

James decides to come clean: to tell Mr Teflon that there were so many things he had learnt since he had started on this contract, so many things that should have been done differently. He decides to show Mr Teflon that there was a better way, to take all the coaching he had experienced through this book, and show him what matters. He has arrived at the 'review' stage. This was going to take a lot of courage - using your influence to 'manage up' was never meant to be easy. But it could be done.

Stage Four ("Review")

We have now reached the fourth stage of the contract methodology, called 'Review'. Let's refer back to the contract management methodology:

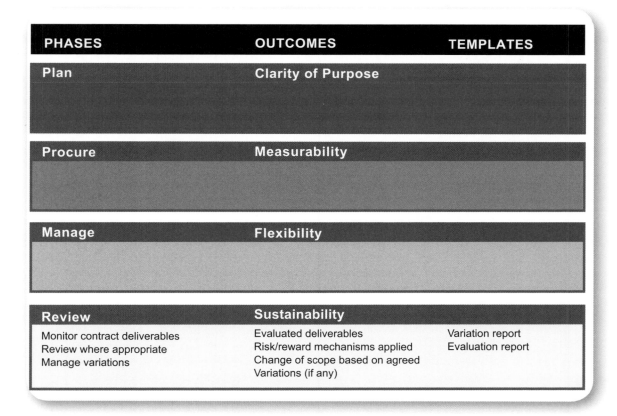

PHASES	OUTCOMES	TEMPLATES
Plan	**Clarity of Purpose**	
Procure	**Measurability**	
Manage	**Flexibility**	
Review	**Sustainability**	
Monitor contract deliverables	Evaluated deliverables	Variation report
Review where appropriate	Risk/reward mechanisms applied	Evaluation report
Manage variations	Change of scope based on agreed Variations (if any)	

Figure 3d: Contract management methodology phase four template.

The 'review' stage will equip you (and James) with tools and techniques to manage some of the curliest parts of the process, including:

- ✓ Managing changes to the contract, usually called 'Variations'
- ✓ How and when to review contractual terms and conditions
- ✓ How to evaluate results on contract completion, in terms of achieving objectives.

Let's examine each of these three processes systematically, as they hold equal weight in stage four – the 'Review' stage of contract management methodology.

Managing contract change

Generally speaking, it's inevitable that some things will change throughout the duration of a contract, particularly longer-term contracts. The balance between sticking to the agreed terms, or varying them in order to suit a new set of circumstances or altered environment lends itself to debate; particularly when there are significant impacts as a consequence of such variations, in terms of time, cost or quality.

Changes for improvement should be embraced rather than shunned. The only way to manage the risk of change is to set up a flexibility mechanism to ensure that as and when change requests arise, there is an agreed process with which to assess them.

However, in order to embrace change, the process to make the changes needs to be understood by everyone and fair and equitable. The last thing you want to set up is a prohibitive complex process to stifle innovation and put any change in the 'too hard basket'.

The variation clause (se Chapter 5) is traditionally written to prevent variations to the contract sneaking up on you, without your consent, or, as the clause usually says, 'unless agreed in writing by the parties'.

Impact

When considering any change to a contract, make your decisions based on the level of impact arising. It's the consequences of the change that matter and need to be considered in full before any change is made.

Mechanism for managing variations

Traditionally, the supplier is always looking to classify changes to a contract as 'variations' to the contract and therefore out of scope, and subject to added charges. On the other side of the contract the procurers purchasers is always looking to contain any variations so that the agreed terms do not change and cost them more money.

This controlling approach tends to stifle innovation. That's not to say that the floodgates should be opened to any variation demand requested by a supplier, but that there should be a mechanism for change in place which can be deployed as and when the need to consider a variation or change arises.

A simple and effective tool that makes it easy to manage change is the variation filter. This acts as a flexibility mechanism in your negotiations. The philosophy behind it is to:

- ✓ Expect change;
- ✓ Embrace change; and
- ✓ Have a process in place to filter change.

The Variation Filter[1]

There are three simple steps in this variation filter tool:

1   HONIG, 1999

1. Variation triggers: The first step is to set up the triggers which will define an 'allowable variation'. An 'allowable' variation is one which, when requested to happen by either party, will constitute a variation for consideration. That means, if a variation does not fall within this definition, it will not be considered for decision making.

2. Priority rating of triggers: Depending on the type of contract and the objectives, the list of possible triggers can be listed and prioritised. The prioritisation of the triggers shows the significance of the change to the actual contract. So in the following template 11 it shows that variations in time would have the greatest impact and so would be the least allowable in terms of the go ahead to make the change.

3. Criteria for accepting variations: The third step is to set up criteria for each of the prioritised variations, allowing for a framework within which decisions can be made, examples of which are listed below:

Priority rating (order of significance of impacts, where 1 would have the greatest impact so least allowable)	Allowable' change triggers (Impacts)	Criteria for accepting variations
E.g. 1	Time	E.g. no more than 7 + days' change
E.g. 2	Cost	E.g. no more than 10% variation
E.g. 3	Quality	E.g. + 5 % tolerance
E.g. 4	Increased risks/issues	
E.g. 5	Change to outcomes (benefits)	
E.g. 6	Change to outputs (deliverables)	

Template 11: *Variation trigger rating tool.*

By having such a process in place, a contract manager can feel comfortable that he/she can handle any change requests as and when they arise, and feel enabled to make decisions within this framework, without having to always seek approval through the organisation's hierarchy. It could also be made transparent to the other party, if you like, so as to have a shared understanding of processes and decision making.

How and when to review contractual terms and conditions

The second element to stage four of the contract management methodology is the actual reviewing of contractual terms.

Contracts usually have clauses in them that state the terms of the contract (period of currency) and whether or not the term can be renewed or reviewed. On a typical contract of two years, there may be an option for either party to renew the contract for a second or third term by agreement.

These are renewed by exercising 'options for renewal', usually to be exercised within six months before the end of the contract. Often, if these options are not renewed, the supplier may lose their right to renew the contract.

In addition to the extension of contract terms by agreement, there may also be review clauses in the contract that increase price or cost of a good or service by CPI or 10%, for example. CPI is the Consumer Price Index, which is usually a minimum increase based on the measure of the change in prices paid by an average household for goods and services for consumption purposes.

Look out for how the contract is supposed to be reviewed and when, as all reviews are accumulative in nature. This means that if the price of the good/ service increases by CPI or 10% each year, by the end of year five there could be substantial increase, and then you may be wanting to renew the contract, which would be based on that now increased price.

How to evaluate results on contract completion

The third part of the 'review' stage entails reflecting on the contract life and deliverables and deciphering where you went right, where you could have improved, the benefits achieved and whether you would use the same suppliers next time or refer them on to others.

A contract evaluation report

The purpose of the evaluation report is to:

✓ identify the strengths and opportunities for improvement in relation to the conduct of the contract management and its deliverables

✓ encourage the contract team to reflect on, and discuss the success of the contract, and

✓ document lessons learned so that they can be applied to future contracts and used to continually build your companies' contract management capabilities.

The contract evaluation report allows you to be introspective and evaluate all the tools and techniques that have been covered in previous chapters. The main two tables you can use to critically assess whether the contract deliverables met the agreed performance standards, as outlined in the contract, are the Reality Checking table (Template 12) and a Lessons Learned at Contract Completion table (Template 13).

After doing a reality check, perhaps in a group workshop, use the table below to describe successful aspects of the contract and areas where the contract could have been improved. This will allow future contract teams to benefit from what worked, whilst at the same time avoid any similar problems.

Performance Standards	Record of Discussion with Contract Team
Outputs and Outcome(s)	• Have the contract parties delivered the outputs? • Has the contract realised the expected outcome(s) and business benefits?
Stakeholders	• Are the clients satisfied? • Are the stakeholders supportive/where they adequately engaged?
Timelines	• Were the deliverables delivered on time? • Did the parties meet all their commitments/milestones?
Budget	• Was the contract delivered within budget?
Quality	• Did the contract deliverables meet the required quality standards?
Risks/Issues	• Did the contract team successfully manage the contract's risks? • What issues arose that could have been avoided?

Template 12: Reality checking table

Phases	What worked well?	What could have been improved?
Plan Stage	• Describe any activities, processes or results which worked well, including any unexpected benefits. • Explain how these could be adapted, shared and used in future projects.	• Describe any activities, processes or results which did not work as planned or had unexpected problems. • Explain how these problems could be reduced or impacted if the project was repeated.
Procure Stage		
Manage		
Stage		
Review Stage		
Risks/ Issues		

Template 13: Lessons learned at contract completion table

CASE STUDY #5: Building for sustainability
"Making the change...for good!"

The business problem

Shopping Centres United Ltd (SCUL) was building a series of multipurpose buildings, including retail shops and residential units, in the newly developed Docklands area. It had previously only built and owned regional shopping centres, but with the rise of development opportunities in the new Docklands, it seized the opportunity to use its capital and take advantage of a new untapped catchments area in a growth corridor.

SCUL had sound project management skills, excellent capabilities in leasing and marketing, and a strong engineering team of technical experts. With their enthusiasm to build and develop, they sometimes neglected the project review stages of contracts, leaving little time to reflect and learn from past projects for future projects. They knew this was a weakness but hadn't done anything about it due to what they called lack of resources for post implementation reviews.

Variations

Following along the same code of behaviour was the way SCUL managed its construction contracts. It never allowed for contingencies or variations in their contracts, based on its philosophy that such things were invented by contractors and were basically the warts or parasites on the contractual agreement. Many new executives didn't agree with this philosophy, but it was hardwired into the company approach and difficult to turn around, involving lawyers, meetings and workshops -- it *was far easier to go along with it. 'We are scoring goals anyway, so why change what's not broken?' said one of their most seasoned and veteran business heads when questioned by a new recruit.*

The Variation that wouldn't go away

One such multipurpose complex that SCUL was building was to be their jewel in their crown. It had 889 residential units, each built like a palace with state-of-the-art design and no expenses spared fittings. The development comprised 800 retail shops, and 989 offices. The building was constructed by the best architects, with interior designers that cost as much as the marble inlays and gold statuettes in the lobbies.

Needless to say, costs blew out, right out into the water on which the buildings were abutting. In fact, in addition to significant cost overruns was a structural problem - the adjacent water banks were not secured in their foundations due to some technicality in conservational and heritage regulations.

Everyone was blaming everyone else. The designers blamed the engineers, SCUL blamed the lawyers and builders started to claim variation payments. The risk management team was called to task because they should have raised this possibility at the beginning of the contract process, which then should have been relayed to the lawyers who then could have incorporated clauses in the contract to cover such an occurrence taking place

Results

SCUL's jewel in the crown was all but ruined. They didn't anticipate such an occurrence, and with safety issues arising they had to act quickly. In the end, the building engineers rectified the problems, costing SCUL in the millions of dollars in compensation to builders and other suppliers, as well as aggrieved buyers and tenants waiting to move into their properties.

SCUL decided to review its policy on variations and tie a new approach to their risk management procedures.

Questions:

1. Apart from the obvious engineering judgment errors made, how could SCUL build in variation management to prevent or forecast such problems happening in future contracts?

2. Using the variation trigger rating tool in Template 11, what two allowable change triggers would you recommend that SCUL incorporate into their planning regime, and how would you prioritise each trigger?

3. Which two corresponding criteria for accepting variations would you then advise be adopted?

4. Would you use the variation management tool as an internal tool only, or something you would share between vendors and suppliers?

How to evaluate results on contract completion

If you believe it should be shared, would you suggest it be reflected and written into the contract?

3. How would you recommend contractual terms be set up, reviewed or varied in SCUL's standard service contracts to prevent such a calamity happen again?

4. At what stage should the variation management process be planned, on commencement of the contracts or before terms and conditions have been finalised?

5. Discuss the example in template 13, and different ways of populating and using the tool.

Priority Rating (1= greatest impact so least allowable)	'Allowable' Change Triggers (impacts)	Criteria for Accepting Variations
1	Quality	E.g. safety codes And no more than $10% variation
2	Increased risks/issues	Zero tolerance to all strategic risks Requires approval from head of risk management
3	Cost	E.g. + 5 % tolerance
4	Time	+ 12 months
5	Change to outcomes (benefits)	0
6	Change to outputs (deliverables)	Subject to quality and risk issues

Template 13: Example of using the internal 'variation trigger rating' tool.

Chapter 10
Lessons to be learned

This chapter sums up the key messages of the book and poses some new thoughts in line with these applied lessons, such as

- ✓ How the contract framework works when time is pressured
- ✓ Using influence to manage your way through the process
- ✓ Conversations you need to have with your partners/stakeholders and managers

We have completed our journey through the contract management framework and methodology. The roadmap is for you to use to streamline your contract management activities and strategic capabilities throughout your organisation.

By this stage, James our friendly contract manager, has turned around to his boss and managed to influence some serious changes to the way he conducts business. No matter what, our friend James will be better equipped and more confident to manage his way through the contract process next time.

This book explains why contract management is a logical process, and how putting a structure to the whole thing really makes contract management easier and more rewarding. If you view contract management as a holistic discipline, from planning to procurement through to managing, negotiating and review/renewing, then the outcomes and benefits of the contract should translate into progress management improvement (PMI) the new wave of change management. Progress management improvement is the equivalent to 'next practice', beyond the 'best practice' of change management.

Let's re-examine some of the steps we went through during the book. Template 14 below is predicated on a powerful set of models making up a framework that completes the contract management model.

The 8-step leading change model

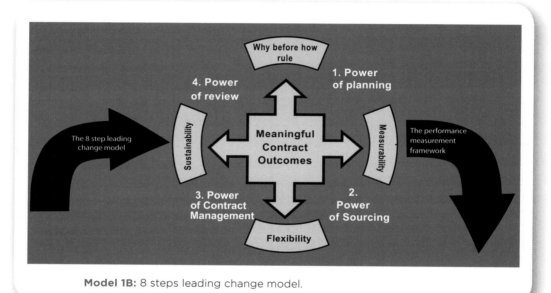

Model 1B: 8 steps leading change model.

Power of Planning
1. Why Before How Rule
2. Build flexibility into Contract Planning
3. Contract Management Model

Power of Sourcing
4. Selection and Care
5. Turning why into how: Measurable and Meaningful

Power of Contract Management

6. High frequency communication, transparent and flexible negotiations

7. Managing contracts for sustainability. Sensitivities to stakeholders needs.

Power of review

8. The stickiness factor: review, renew, rewind/vary

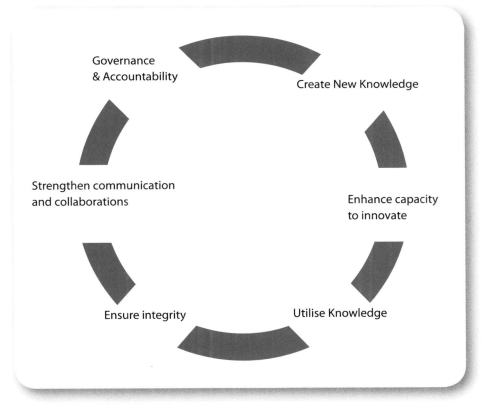

Template 14: The performance measurement framework

There are four stages to the contract management lifecycle:

✓ Plan }working ON the process
✓ Procure }
✓ Manage }working IN the process
✓ Review }

The leading contract management four power model sets out four main principles to underpin the stages:

✓ Stage 1: Plan (Principle 1: Clarity of Purpose)
✓ Stage 2: Procure (Principle 2: Measurability)
✓ Stage 3: Manage (Principle 3: Flexibility)
✓ Stage 4: Review (Principle 4: Sustainability)

The contract management methodology shows a structure to the framework, which is measured through achieving a series of staged outcomes, and managed through a series of solid templates and models (see figure 3).

One of the most important things in contract management is not only to understand the contract in layman's terms, but to share that understanding with all parties, including and particularly the accountability of roles and responsibilities. There are philosophical and functional reasons for contracting out, and as long as everyone is on the 'same page' with regards to these reasons, the relationship will head out on the right path.

Using the contract proposal form (see Template 1, Chapter 2) before anything is procured, enables you to work out why you need to contract out, your objectives and proposed benefits (outcomes) and deliverables (outputs).

Working out 'who' (who you select to contract to and with) should involve identifying your 'best-fit' supplier in a multi-dimensional exercise, best represented by our best-fit scorecard in Chapter 3. Best-fit supplier score carding takes into account cultural fit as well as many other factors (Template 2). The cultural mapping exercise (Chapter 4) is designed to guide you through this curly decision making path. As long as you know which way you want to head, and understand your own cultural expectations and needs, the curliness can get ironed out to allow you to make a decision.

Once you know what's what, which supplier you need that is best-fit for purpose, you can then use the value-for-money model (chapter 3) and examine its true meaning, including your supplier capabilities, their actual offer, whole of life costs, and the strategic marketplace.

Two key templates in the planning stage are the contract management plan (Template 3), and the transition plan (based on figure 8). Planning for success is your first key to managing for value-add and mutual benefits.

The next stage in contract management is working out what you consider to be success. The performance measurement wheel (figure 15, Chapter 6) takes a strategic view of measurement, something we should all be doing during the procurement stage in order to manage contracts better and make them work. The performance measurement wheel starts well before governance and accountability is measured. It commences at measuring the creation of new knowledge, given that knowledge management is our biggest challenge in a growing world of information overload.

Relationship management is one of the key risk mitigation strategies around, and the key to relationship management is understanding what behaviours you need to adopt to get along with people who do not share your core emotional drives. Relationship management is the key to managing your way through a contract process, and negotiating like a partner, rather than like 'the other side'.

The 8-step leading change model

Negotiation is an ongoing process, starting well before the supplier is procured, and continuing on throughout the entire contract management lifecycle. Setting out a useful and workable negotiation strategy can be expedited by the template set out in figure 17. Take particular note of the BATNA (your 'Best Alternative for a Negotiated Agreement') referred to there, which acts as an insurance policy in case your worst-case scenario is not achieved during any one negotiation.

The fourth stage of the contract managment methodolgy, the review stage, encompasses:

- ✓ Managing change to contract terms and conditions;
- ✓ Reviewing the terms; and
- ✓ Evaluating the contract on completion.

When examining whether changes – or variations – are to be made, the best test is in the impact assessment test, working out what could happen if the change was – or wasn't – made. The philosophy underpinning this assessment is to:

1. Expect change;
2. Embrace change; and
3. Have a process in place to filter change.

The variation filter model and variation trigger rating tool (see Template 11, Chapter 9) is a simple user-friendly tool that underpins a process for decision making when confronted with a variation. It involves first defining change in terms of triggers (ie what the parties agree to define as a variation) and then set a series of criteria for making a decision to accept or decline the variation once the implications (impacts) are considered.

Finally, when a contract is completed – or indeed if it is terminated – it should be evaluated by the contract manager, procurement manager and key stakeholders to review what was done well, what could have been improved and what lessons to publish for the rest of the organisation. This exercise should also be carried out even in the event of a contract renewal. Oftentimes, this could also be shared with suppliers and other stakeholders so as to allow next practice to be embedded into best practice in the way.

In summary, seek to develop specific skills as a contract manager to manage your way through the process, and help manage others for a better developed cycle. Contract management roles are set out in Chapter 1 figure 5a, and related skills are set out in figure 5b.

Figure 19 (below) is an overview success factor governance tool that examines the steps within the framework as a checklist.

Critical success factors governance tool

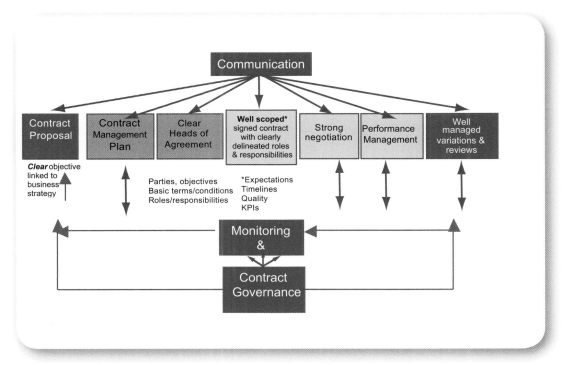

Figure 19: Critical success factors governance tool.

You could use this critical success factors tool by thinking of a contract you are managing or about to manage at work, and take a moment to give your contract a score out of 10 based on the contract management governance profile above. Each box in the diagram carries one point out of 10. Your overall score shows where you are doing well, and where you need to improve. Use the scoring sheet as follows:

Score
- ☐ Contract proposal
- ☐ Contract management plan
- ☐ Clarified heads of agreement
- ☐ Well scoped, signed contract
- ☐ Strong negotiation
- ☐ Performance management in place
- ☐ Well managed variations and reviews
- ☐ Strong communication
- ☐ Performance monitoring and feedback mechanisms in place
- ☐ Sound contract governance (accountability and risk management)

$\overline{10}$

What factors need working on? What's your contract score out of 10 marks?

Contract management checklist

Checklists are important to make sure you haven't forgotten anything, so here is a snapshot of the contract management checklist for a full run through just before you commence a contract.

Finally, this book ends on the same note where we began. It's all about how you work with people. Making relationships work will make your commercial contract work. At all stages in the contract management process you need to:

✓ be clear and transparent about your objectives and understand your supplier objectives

✓ focus on the people issues

✓ make long-term decisions (businesses have long memories)

✓ focus, within a globally 'flattened' world, on cultural differences - embrace them, and use them to create stronger results and better more fulfilling outcomes

You are now equipped with knowledge, tools and techniques. Go out there and share your wisdom, apply the knowledge and be a better change agent. Contract management is about creating sustainable change, which should make your business a better, more sustainable entity. Happy contracting!

Plan
Preparation of Contract
Proposal
Draft EOI, RFT

Procure
Maintenance of records of procurement
• Heads of agreement
• Contract management plan
• Transition plan
• Contract
• Assign staff and allocate resources

Manage
Review contract performance: progress and compliance
Communicate with contractors to maximise performance in line with strategic intent
Payment plan in line with contract provisions and applicable law for standards
Maintenance of records:
• Status reporting
• Incentive/penalty payments
• Risk log and communications plan
• Negotiation Strategy
• Subcontractor monitoring

Review
Evaluation of contract deliverables
(in terms of achievement of organisational objectives)

Variations management:
• Change of scope
• Variations report
• Evaluation report

Figure 20: Contract management checklist.

Contract management checklist

Index

About the Author

Beverley Honig, BA, LLB, MBA

Beverley Honig is well-known in industry circles as a strategic change manager, a business developer, and a lawyer with a wealth of experience in Australia, England and the Middle East. With many years of general management experience under her belt with companies such as Coles Myer Ltd, she brings unique commercial executive experience working with and growing billion dollar asset portfolios.

Armed with an MBA from the number one business school in the AsiaPacific, she has grown Honeylight Enterprises over the past decade to be a leading change management consultancy, specialising in people management matters with a focus on corporate and industry growth and sustainability. Beverley has been invited to join many government, public and private boards due to her people and property experience that enables business improvement and growth. Her diverse portfolio of board appointments includes: Board Director Centre for Adult Education, Director of Melbourne Markets Authority, Chairman of Occupational English Testing Board, Director of Australian Chamber of Commerce, and Chairman/Judge of Essential Service Commission - Appeals.

Beverley is an expert in the field of business planning and development, and advises a long list of clients--from private and public companies to Government bodies--on how to focus and develop their business through good business planning and practice. Within her portfolio of services she specialises in strategic procurement, venture creation, commercial contract management and opening new markets for global companies.

Beverley has written this book based on her extensive successful experience in global training and development programs relating to change management, effective commercial contract management and strategic project management.

Beverley is a globally sought after public speaker, and a lecturer at Monash University. She was honoured for her achievements by being nominated in 1997 for the awards of IWFCI/Drake International Businesswomen of the year and Telstra Business Women of the Year. In 2005, 2006 and again in 2007 Honeylight Enterprises received the prestigious Trade Award, which is bestowed by the Prime Minister, in recognition of an outstanding contribution in the forging of international trade links. Beverley is listed in the Who's Who of Australia. See more on www.honeylight.com.au.

Please share your thoughts and insights, successes and other stories with the author, Beverley Honig, by email via www.honeylight.com.au.

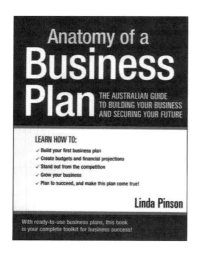

Other Business Titles by Woodslane Press

Mastering Incoming Sales Calls

Author: Nigel Allan

Every time someone calls a business they have chosen that organisation as a possible supplier of something they want. Each incoming call is not just a possible customer, but a probable customer. Converting them into sales can be easy, but only if you manage the calls properly! This book focuses exclusively on the hitherto largely ignored area of dealing with incoming calls, and dealing with them in a way that will allow business owners, managers and sales staff to get face-to-face opportunities to sell their products. It includes step-by-step examples and case studies to show exactly how to become a `Phone Master'. The reader will be able to create and follow presentations, and see why up to 96% of the top salespeople in the world use a planned presentation when using the telephone.

RRP: $29.99 • **ISBN:** 9781921203800

Hiring & Firing

Author: John Grant

This book deals with the complex issues of Australian employment law in a straightforward and matter of fact way. All the issues that come up in the daily process of running a business are presented in the language of the business owner. Supported by templates for letters and contracts ready to download and use on the accompanying CD, this book will keep owners and managers out of the employment tribunal and focused on running their businesses. John Grant, cut his teeth in the Arbitration and Conciliation commission on behalf of the Australian Workers Union. Combining his legal practice with journalism he has focused on the issues he understands best.

RRP: $39.95 • **ISBN:** 9781875889846

Woodslane Press can be contacted by:

Email: info@woodslane.com.au • **www.woodslaneonline.com.au**
Phone: (02) 9970 5111 • **Fax:** (02) 9970 5002

Other Business Titles by Woodslane Press

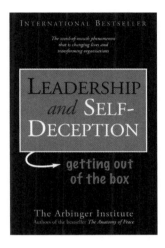

Leadership and Self-Deception

Author: The Arbinger Institute

Leadership and Self-Deception reveals that there are only two ways for leaders to be: the source of leadership problems or the source of leadership success. The authors examine this surprising truth, identify self-deception as the underlying cause of leadership failure. Through an entertaining and highly instructive story Leadership and Self-Deception clearly demonstrates how people can stop undermining themselves and what amazing things happen when they do - freely and fully putting to work all the behavioural skills, systems, and techniques that will bring success to them and their organizations.

RRP: $29.99 • **ISBN:** 9781921203527

Persuasion & Influence

Author: Bruce Hilliard

Moving away from the traditional hit-and-miss methods of persuasion, this book applies real science to fundamental business and life skills. From a business perspective, the very practical process described in this book allows anyone to rapidly create a truly persuasive message, that is very easy to understand, and highly influential. Additionally, the techniques can be used for almost any endeavour where you need to clearly convey and important message. This is the power of the universal principles described in this book.

RRP: $49.95 • **ISBN:** 9781921606663

Woodslane Press can be contacted by:

Email: info@woodslane.com.au • **www.woodslaneonline.com.au**

Phone: (02) 9970 5111 • **Fax:** (02) 9970 5002

Feedback and Registration

We do hope that you have found this book useful, but we know that nothing in this world is perfect and your suggestions for improving future editions would be much appreciated.

Even if you have no comment on this current edition but would like to register, you will be sent occasional information on pertinent new books (both printed and those new to e-format) and will also be sent free pdf update notes as and when they become necessary for this edition.

Your name: _____

Your address or email address: _____

_____

Your contact phone (optional): _____

What you most liked about Making Contracts Work: _____

_____

_____

What you least liked about the book:_____

_____

_____

Please tick below and return this form (or simply email us the salient details) if you would like to be kept informed of Woodslane's products and services:

☐ pdf update notes for this book

☐ notifications of new editions of this book

☐ details of other business books published by Woodslane Press

☐ details of other business books distributed by Woodslane

☐ details of other computer-user books distributed by Woodslane

Woodslane Press can be contacted by:
Email: info@woodslane.com.au • **www.woodslaneonline.com.au**
Phone: (02) 9970 5111 • **Fax:** (02) 9970 5002